Mary Flaherty
1981

WOMAN'S
ESTATE

Juliet Mitchell

WOMAN'S ESTATE

If I e'er Grow to Man's Estate,
O, Give to me a Woman's fate!
May I govern all, both great and small,
Have the last word and take the wall.
  WILLIAM BLAKE

VINTAGE BOOKS
A Division of Random House
New York

VINTAGE BOOKS EDITION, April 1973
Library of Congress Cataloging in Publication Data
Mitchell, Juliet, 1940–
    Woman's estate.
    Includes bibliographical references.
    1. Women's Liberation Movement. 2. Woman—
History and condition of women. I. Title.
[HQ1154.M53   1973]   301.41'2   72–10106
ISBN 0-394-71905-0
Manufactured in the United States of America

For Otti

Contents

Acknowledgements

My thanks are due, above all, to the Women's Liberation Movement for what it will do for all women in the future, and for what it has already done for so many of us.

I also wish to thank the *New Left Review* for permission to reprint (in somewhat altered form) an article I wrote in 1966: 'Women: The Longest Revolution' (*N L R* no. 40); *Modern Occasions* for an extract from my review of Kate Millet's *Sexual Politics* ('The Sexual Revolution', *Modern Occasions,* Winter 1970); *Shrew* (the magazine of the London Women's Liberation Workshop) for the use of Margaret Walter's article on Holland and for an extract from my own article 'Why Freud?' (*Shrew,* November–December 1970).

I thank, too, André Schiffrin for the suggestion, Florence Hobson for the typing and Marjorie, Eric, Daphne, Margaret, Anna and Jim.

Preface

By 1970 there was some form of Women's Liberation Movement active in all but three of the liberal democratic countries of the advanced capitalist world.[1] The exceptions are Iceland – an isolated enclave of pseudo-egalitarian capitalism – and Austria and Switzerland, in social terms probably the most traditional and hierarchic of European societies. Women's Liberation is an international movement – not in organization, but in its identification and shared goals. This distinguishes it, in part, from its historical predecessors: the suffrage struggles of the late nineteenth and early twentieth centuries.[2] It distinguishes it also from its current media presentation as an Anglo-Saxon, predominantly American movement. In England, this insular presentation serves the function of assimilating it to the popular conception of earlier feminism and thus contributes to diffusing its impact: women went wild before, so they are again. It's only a flash-in-the-pan!

Most of the different groups are professedly, if variously, revolutionary.[3] Why are they rarely seen to be such?

1. There are also active groups in Japan, South Africa, Australia, Turkey and Afghanistan; these fall outside the scope of this discussion.

2. The earlier feminists in Britain and the United States had international contacts and did influence each other. There were also important struggles in other countries such as Sweden and Norway. But this did not make it international. The current coincidence of Women's Liberation groups clearly bears analogy with the international nature of the Student Movement.

3. The National Organization of Women (NOW) – the largest of all American groups is reformist and is not now regarded as a part of Women's Liberation either by itself or by most other groups. However, see pp. 72–4 for the importance of non-revolutionary and reformist groups.

Every day in the press or on television in the United States and increasingly in England, there are comments on the movement, or statements from its spokeswomen. As women claim that they want to change the whole structure of society, that they see the system as oppressive and to be combatted at every level, interviewers smile benignly (or scoffingly), clearly envisaging that a 'change in the system' might mean a bit more washing-up or child-minding for the husband. It is true that currently it is a fashionable movement, and that laughter takes the sting out of the attack, and that if verbal aggression escalates into acts of violence then, as it did with the suffragettes, the state's repressive and coercive forces will come into play. Already, it is claimed that in America militant women are losing or not obtaining jobs. There is no reason why violence and counter-violence should not reach the peaks achieved in the first decades of this century in England. Then the suffragettes burnt down houses, smashed shop windows, assaulted Members of Parliament, planted bombs, destroyed over a hundred buildings in a matter of months and disrupted communications by blowing up letter-boxes and cutting telegraph wires. They generally scarred the countryside of England with their demand for the vote. In turn, they were imprisoned, forcibly fed and beaten up. A special Act of Parliament – the 'Cat-and-Mouse' Act – enabled their continual reimprisonment. But while this went on, the headquarters of the most militant group – the Women's Social and Political Union (the W S P U) – with campaign funds of £90,000, one hundred and ten paid staff, a subscribing membership of one thousand and a newspaper circulation of 40,000, remained untouched. True, conspiracy charges were brought against some of the leaders and Christabel Pankhurst was forced into exile, but neither this nor any other organization as such was ever smashed. It is sometimes necessary to shut women up, but their political organizations are never to be taken too seriously.

Today, something comparable seems to be happening. The assimilation of Women's Liberation by the media into colourful reportage may be symptomatic of something more than its hungry lust for sexual objects in any shape they come. As individuals, many men react to women's claims with fear or, alternatively, with bemused, compensatory tolerance. But there is no indication that as yet, despite its enormous growth, the organized movement can claim more than nuisance value. All previous revolutionary movements have had, at their centre, at the crucial times, to be clandestine. It is not just that the media gives Women's Liberation publicity, it is that, in concept and organization, it is the most public revolutionary movement ever to have existed. Able, too, to make the most revolutionary statements in public without anyone seeming bothered. This raises many questions, not only about a society which sees women as always unserious, but perhaps, more critically for the immediate future, about the nature of the movement itself.

We have to ask why it arose (the conditions that timed its birth in the late sixties). What it is like as a political movement. What problems does it have to confront in analysing the position of women. And . . . where do we go from here?

In discussing the historical time at which it arose we have to consider contemporary radical or revolutionary movements with which it is in alliance or from which it broke: the student movement, Black Power, draft resistance, already existent sectarian groups and reformist women's groups, Third World struggles. We have to consider the specific condition of women during the decade that produced the revolt.

A description of the characteristics of the movement involves its size, class-nature and the activity of its participants, its organization, the campaigns it wages and the concepts it is evolving in the process of building itself as a political movement: consciousness-raising, male chauvinism, sexism, feminism, liberationism and its no-leadership structures. Also the revolutionary or radical tradition it draws on: the 'politics of experience',[4] the spontanist methods of anarcho-syndicalism

4. The 'politics of experience' is the term now loosely used to suggest an analysis of society from the perspective of one's self. The experience of personal alienation is the means of testing the total social alienation which is the product of our decaying capitalist society. R. D. Laing's *The Politics*

and the Situationists, the separatism of Black Power, socialist theories of the unity in struggle of oppressed peoples, the concept of itself as a grass-roots, potentially mass movement. Also, of the analysis so far tentatively developed, which in its broadest outlines runs something like – women are an oppressed people, we can learn about this oppression by using the 'politics of experience', we can combat oppression by attacking the agents and institutions of power (men and/or male-dominated society) to produce either 'equality' or the 'liberated self': 'whole people'.[5]

We have also to discuss the specific features of woman's situation that most clearly locate her oppression. Quite simply, how do we analyse the position of women? What is the woman's concrete situation in contemporary capitalist society? What is the universal or general area which defines her oppression? The family and the psychology of femininity are clearly crucial here. However inegalitarian her situation at work (and it is invariably so) it is within the development of her feminine psyche and her ideological and socio-economic role as mother and housekeeper that woman finds the oppression that is hers alone. As this defines her, so any movement for her liberation must analyse and change this position.

Where are we going? Quite simply, is the movement which claims to be revolutionary in intention moving towards the formation of itself as a revolutionary organization? What would this mean in terms of its internal structure and external alliances? Is the feminist concept of women as the most fundamentally oppressed people and hence potentially the most revolutionary to be counterposed to the Marxist position

---

of Experience and The Bird of Paradise, is perhaps a focal point for this notion: 'No one can begin to think, feel or act now except from the starting point of his or her own alienation. . . . Humanity is estranged from its authentic possibilities. . . . We are born into a world where alienation awaits us. . . . Alienation as our present destiny is achieved only by outrageous violence perpetrated by human beings on human beings' (pp. 11–12). The 'politics of experience' fuses the personal and the political.

5. For a discussion of the notion of 'whole people' see Sheila Rowbotham: *Women's Liberation and the New Politics,* published by the Bertrand Russell Foundation and The May Day Manifesto, 1970.

of the working class as *the* revolutionary class under capitalism? If so, with what consequences? What is the relationship between class-struggle and the struggles of the oppressed? What *are* the politics of oppression?

Part One

THE WOMEN'S
LIBERATION MOVEMENT

Chapter One

The Background of the Sixties

Women's Liberation and Previous Feminist Struggles

What were the origins of the Women's Liberation Movement? Why did it arise in the second half of the sixties?

The movement is assimilated to the earlier feminist struggles of the nineteenth and early twentieth century, not only, as I have mentioned, by external analysts, but also by itself. This obscures its novelty. Naturally the first and latest feminist protest movements bear resemblances – but it is important that these are within their characteristics rather than in their origins. Just as in the United States the nineteenth-century Abolitionist movement was different from Civil Rights and Black Power, the feminist struggles that, in part, evolved from these are different. This distinction is more than just a hotting-up of the battle: qualitively different relationships between the women and the black emancipators (or black fighters) developed. Even at a merely symptomatic level this is true: the nineteenth-century feminists discovered the prejudices (and more) of their own dominant white men and their government; with Stokeley Carmichael's famous putting down of women to a 'prone' position in the revolutionary movement, women in the 1960s found the attitude of the oppressor within the minds of the oppressed. This, among many other factors, has led to the analysis offered by groups of radical feminists: the overthrow of male-dominated society (sexism) and the liberation of women is the primary revolution. Racism itself is only an off-shoot of sexism.[1]

1. See Shulamith Firestone's analysis of racism in *The Dialectic of Sex*, Jonathan Cape, 1971. I discuss some of the implications of her argument on pp. 87–96.

In Sweden, a different experience, the assimilation of the earlier feminist struggle to a continuous emancipatory movement, government-approved, was, I think, a brake on the growth of a militant movement. The first and most recent stages of the struggle are clearly to be very different.

In England, again, there are comparable conditions for the 'first' and 'second' feminist 'phase': the decline of Liberal England in the first decade of the century has its parallels in the death gasps of Labour's swan-song in the sixties; both epochs were marked by a virulent right-wing rebellion (e.g. Enoch Powell), by violent rebellion in the nearest colony, Ireland, and by a powerful women's movement. But the militant suffragettes and the more moderate suffragists found an issue that unified them into existence and simultaneously led them right out of any revolutionary possibilities – the vote. The slogans of feminists today may seem no more radical than those of spokeswomen in the past, but the context alters the meaning.

It is this context we have to consider: the specific political background of the 1960s.

Radicalism in the Sixties

Broadly speaking, the mid-sixties in the advanced capitalist world were characterized by the struggles of three related but distinct groups: Blacks, Students (and high-school children) and Youth (the Hippies in all their variations, American Youth International Party – the yippies – and draft resisters). Of course, not every country had all movements. These home-based, home-directed fights took over from a preoccupation with world peace and Third World struggles – Algeria, Cuba, Vietnam – yet have never lost the predilection for internationalism that their original inspiration provided. This internationalism has gone in two directions: the general and abstract quality of ban-the-bomb has nestled into the timeless void of peace-of-mind – meditation unites mankind. It is encapsulated in the simplicities of the world as a global village, it echoes from the feet of Hippies migrating to Kashmir – and back again. The Third World revolutions and guerrilla warfare provoked new analyses of oppression and new methods of struggle; Blacks are the Vietnamese within America itself. The Women's Liberation Movement is, in a sense, a summation of so many tendencies that still mark these slightly earlier formations.

The wish to concentrate on specific oppression in one's own country and yet link it up with a universal predicament (a reaction to the scope of imperialism?) finds perfect expression in the situation of women. The exploitation of women in the advanced societies is easy to document; its alliance with their oppression everywhere and at all times is evident. Women are the most 'international' of any political group, and yet their oppression is experienced in the most minute and specific area – in the home. The confluence of the personal and the political. Though some women are maintained to a high standard, the vast majority share with Blacks (and the working class) social and economic poverty; they share with students an experience of ideological manipulation and with Hippies they can protest the society's repression or exploitation of sexuality, its denial of freedom and their search for it within the resources of the individual. But the very breadth and all-inclusiveness of women's oppression presents complications. Like Blacks, most women are poor, yet like students and Youth revolutionaries, the women in the movement are largely middle-class. It is the implications of this combination that we have to discover in tracing back the origins of Women's Liberation.

Women's Liberation had revolutionary food from two sources: women's economic poverty within the richest country in the world (like the Blacks) and their mental and emotional debasement in some of the richest conditions that country provides (like students and youth). A growing consciousness of the latter permitted the realization of the former.

For poverty alone cannot protest for itself. It is never extreme deprivation that produces the revolutionary. William Hinton, in *Fanshen*, describes the abysmal conditions of life in

pre-revolutionary Shansi Province of China, an almost un-
believable account of brutality and degradation.

By the second quarter of the twentieth century these (social) relations and (natural) conditions had reduced Southern Shansi to a
nadir of rapacious exploitation, structural decay, chronic violence
and recurring famine which has few parallels in history . . .[2]

Yet it is not from the nadir that revolutions can come: it is
from the prospect, not of a summit (Utopianism), but at least
of a hill that can be ascended. American women and students
were far away from the Shansi peasants at the bottom of the
well (their phrase and Hinton's); but the gap between the
deprivation they suffered and glory they were supposed to
enjoy was sufficiently startling for them to challenge both. It
is from this position of a prospect that all the revolutionary
movements of the sixties in the advanced capitalist societies
emerged.

Seen from this perspective, the 'middle-class' composition
of Women's Liberation is not an unhappy fact, a source of
anxiety and endless 'mea culpas' but an intrinsic part of
feminist awareness. The most economically and socially under-
privileged woman is bound much tighter to her condition by
a consensus which passes it off as 'natural'. An Appalachian
mother of fifteen children experiences her situation as 'natural'
and hence inescapable: a college-educated girl spending her
time studying 'home economics' for an academic degree is at
least in a position to ask 'why?'

Oppression is about more than economic exploitation as
even the most economically deprived of the early radical
movements – Black Power – demonstrated.

The Black Movement

Among the earliest expressions of the Black Power struggle
there were decisive cultural attacks. 'Black is beautiful!' and
the whole assertion of Black values have a political significance

2. William Honton: *Fanshen*, Vintage Books, 1966, pp. 67–8.

overlooked in the dismissive attitude that it had merely psychological importance. Perhaps we can best see this significance in the absence of anything equivalent in current
working-class movements; or in the presence of it in the wars
of liberation in the Third World. Despite Lenin's strictures,
working-class struggle in the West has remained too firmly
within the boundaries of its own economic exploitation, tied
either to trade union politics or to the gradualism of reformist
communist parties. The fully-developed political consciousness of an exploited class or oppressed group cannot come
from within itself, but only from a knowledge of the interrelationships (and domination structures) of all the classes
in a society. Blacks do not necessarily have this 'overview' any more than the working-class, but because their
oppression is visibly cultural as well as economic there is an
impetus to see the diverse aspects of oppression within the
whole system. This does *not* mean an immediate comprehension of the ways in which other groups and classes are exploited or oppressed, but it *does* mean what one could call a
'totalist' attack on capitalism which *can* come to realize the
need for solidarity with all other oppressed groups.

The origins of 'totalism' are quite clear. As is its necessity.
The inspiration is the struggle of the Third World countries
against imperialist oppression; a total struggle for the survival
of a nation and a culture. Blacks see their position as that of a
Third World enclave within the homeland of imperialism.
The first stages of struggle were, thus, the reassertion of
nationhood – a Black country within America. But the truth of
this is only analogous. Blacks are historically too late, geo-
graphically too dispersed, numerically too few to fight this
battle. They are not the sole victims of total imperialist aggression like the Vietnamese; they are the most grossly exploited and oppressed minority within a capitalist system. The
'totalist' position is a precondition for this realization, but it
must diversify its awareness or get stuck in the mud of Black
chauvinism, which is a racial and cultural equivalent of working-class economism, seeing no further than one's own badly
out-of-joint nose. What is true of workers is no less true of
Blacks:

Working-class consciousness cannot be genuine political consciousness unless the workers are trained to respond to *all* cases of
tyranny, oppression, violence, and abuse, no matter *what class* is
affected.[3]

Imperialist-capitalism, the colossus with the feet of clay,
the paper tiger, is still a tiger, still a colossus, and no oppressed
group can go it alone.

'Totalism', then, is the expression of the protest against all
oppressed conditions in the form of an assertion of complete
liberation involving the overthrow at one blow of the whole of
capitalist society. In 'totalism' the oppression of one group
stands for the oppression of all. Within its undifferentiated
inclusiveness there is only place for tactics, not overall strategy.
However, it is an important early stage in the organization
against an oppression which is as much manifest in social and
cultural repression as in exploitation. 'Totalism' applies to
the feminist struggle as it does to the Black.

The Black struggle, then, made the first stand for the inclusiveness of oppression. But few Black militants were
initially middle-class. In protesting the experience of middle-
class deprivation, women found themselves closer to the
student movement in which many of them had participated.

Students

For Lenin, the poor students of autocratic Russia were one of
a number of oppressed groups. The present-day Student
Movement, at least its Marxist components, tried urgently to
recapture this self-definition. Students, they claimed, were not
the privileged enclave that a complacent society saw itself as
generously providing, they were the new poor, a new part of
the working-class. I am not concerned for the moment with
the viability of this argument, rather with how it came to be
made possible, and with its implications. Lenin's students
were poor and hence radical: the students of the 1960s were

3. V. I. Lenin: *What Is To Be Done*', Moscow, 1964, p. 66.

radicals and hence saw clearly their own poverty. Yet, whether living on state stipends, loans, their own part-time work or on their parents, it still remained true that students came, in the overwhelming majority, from (white) middle-class homes, and these were, largely, where they were returning. Any actual poverty they suffered was temporary. Their protest, then, did not come out of economic exploitation or oppression. It came out of a new definition of the latter. What is interesting is that both the students and the middle-class women of Women's Liberation have open to them many possibilities of all the available education and wealth. It is these they have rejected as 'poor'. Obviously this is a complex assertion.

Really until the Second World War, students in the Arts subjects were an intellectual élite, studying for its own sake, with future work connected to the status of being a graduate, rather than to the content of the University Degree pursued. The future work of science and technical students was always more related to their university course. Other professional jobs had their own training – separate from universities – lawyers, doctors, accountants, journalists, and so on. Gradually, since the war, but far more acutely during the sixties, the position of students in the Arts subjects has been shifting out of its ivory tower possibilities into a situation much more analogous to that previously applicable only to scientists and technicians. Arts students have had to professionalize themselves into media-men or advertising copy-writers in a booming media industry. The university has become the training ground for agents of the consumer society. Students are no longer students in the classical sense of the term. University courses cling vainly to an inappropriate tradition against whose conservative content students protest, while courses introduced to fit organically into their future jobs reveal a banality that condemns both themselves and those jobs. It is the Arts students who are the vanguard and mainstay of the Student Movement. If not the new workers, they are certainly the new apprentices to a new type of job.

This position of students has bearings on Women's Liberation in two ways. Most simply, a large number of early women's liberationists were and are, students in Arts Faculties. Of more elusive and interesting importance is the shifting socio-economic background which produced the conditions just described. This background made possible the change in the student consciousness and so also affected the position and awareness of middle-class women, enabling them, as it did the students, at least partially to transform their class origins. Precisely from their affluence, both groups were able to move to demand its overthrow. Students claiming to be 'workers' should not be taken to refer simply to their poverty, but rather to the poverty of their affluence, to the compulsion of their much-vaunted 'choice'. And middle-class women are in a similar position: told they are equal, that emancipation has given them everything, that working as housewives 'your time is your own'– lucky to be women, not having the work, the worry and the responsibility ... but.... The position of students and housewives in the eyes of those who are neither is really very analogous: idle and free from responsibility.

It is not, then, that these movements are simply the product of disillusionment: you offered us culture, you offered us leisure, and look what it means. Rather, there is a profound contradiction between the actual work endured and an ideology that denies it.

Students are protesting against their mental and intellectual manipulation within a context – the university – that is supposed to guarantee their freedom.

Hippies and the Politics of Youth

Hippies protest against the social manipulation and repression of emotion. In a world of automation and alienation, they assert that what anyone feels is valid. After all, having been told that all along – why not put such pieties to the test? The Hippy underground initially appropriated the values of freedom, emotionality and the rights of the individual and, by taking them seriously, validated them for the first time. Yet, despite the fact that the Hippies look backwards and forwards

– to past and future 'golden ages' – for the apotheosis of their values, these values are, in fact, inevitably a distorted mirror-reflection of advanced capitalist ideologies. The Hippy community can now often reintegrate into society as a religious enclave – because it has never got outside its own, and the society's, religiosity. Primitive reflective politics of this kind that try to extend the dimensions of the offered values are easily incorporated. Even the apparently 'delinquent' drug-culture used a radical language that was a sad mockery of the available culture – drugs 'expand one's consciousness'; in a slightly different sense, what else does a consumer society want to achieve but to expand the consciousness of needs for the vastly increased sale of a vastly increased number of products? The danger of such vague ideological radicalism is that it remains ideological. Most Hippy groups transcend the capitalist socio-economic order only by inhabiting its more ethereal and timeless realms, ultimately by exploring its most pervasive sell – religion. Opium is the religion of these. . . . Admittedly, carrying anything to its logical conclusion has radical effects. Few bourgeois ideologues initially owned up to their Hippy progeny. And, in their turn, in the process of exploring the freed zone of consciousness, many groups came up with insights and possibilities with revolutionary dimensions.

The counter-cultural parody of the Yippies has yet more radical possibilities. By turning to expose and exploit the media (particularly television), the Yippies at least focus on one manifestation of the ideological terrain on which this battle has to be fought. But it is as yet an uncharted one, and the protest can effervesce into random exuberance. The line between parodying the T.V. show and providing it with a necessary shot-in-the-arm of youthful fun and games is a hard one to draw.

In the unorganized politics that such movements propagate, in their essential absence of leaders and structures, their ultimate effectiveness depends on the political commitment of individuals. . . . Yet at their worst, they are the more-or-less joyful symptoms of a decaying order; at their best, they are the agents or instigators of a new one.

The Shared Background

Education

An essential and dominant aspect of the common context of these movements seems to me to be the vast expansion in higher education in the first half of the sixties. This was partially a response to demographic pressures – the babies of the post-war birth-boom came of college age in 1964 – and also a result of changing economic demands. In America, Black colleges, city and state schools expanded. In England, many technical, educational and art colleges had the greatness of university status thrust upon them in an open arm policy of providing a respectable home for the nation's teeming youth. The population of all the political movements of the sixties is young and likely to be 'educated' – even if, as with Blacks, they are grotesquely under-privileged. It is education and its implications that can explain the problem of the class-nature of the new revolutionaries. For now it seems that there is the potentiality within a greatly increased intellectual sector of middle class for revolutionary impetus on its own behalf. In other words, not acting as an enclave and as leverage within the working-class struggle (i.e. the revolutionary 'role of the intellectual'), but themselves participating as an organic part of that struggle. This is the opposite position from that ideological statement of the embourgeoisement of the working class. What is happening, rather, is that some groups within the traditional working class, the skilled technicians, for instance, and some within the traditional middle class are growing closer together in their class position. This is far from a personal shift up or down the social ladder, it is a symptom of the progress of capitalism itself.

The sheer number of students, in a country like America, in colleges and universities, is an important aspect of an advanced capitalist situation. This is a somewhat different phenomenon from that found in early capitalist societies. During the nineteenth century the increasing complexity of machinery brought a demand for literacy in its wake and, tardily, a compulsory education system. However, what we are witnessing in the expansion of higher education from the early sixties onwards is not just a straight continuation of this earlier development. It is something qualitatively as well as quantitatively different. People are being educated not simply (as is often made out) for the skills required in the increasing complexities of technical production, but also for the expansion of the mental universe itself, a universe that has to be enormously much wider in a society geared to consumption than in one oriented around primary production.[4]

Consumer capitalism depends on the ability to sell and the massive multiplication of the means of selling. For each new product a new advertisement, new copy-writer, new lay-out girl, new transmission operator, a new need in the buyer created by.... The material 'thing' is still paramount, but clearly the whole is 'bottom-heavy'. This in itself is an index of affluence. The greater the development of capital, the higher the rate of reproduction that is necessary to maintain it. People from the colleges and universities are increasingly called in to perform this work – and no longer to undertake traditional intellectual work in 'the professions'. They are the agents of consumer capitalism, themselves the symptom of the development away from the primary production to incessant reproduction and, a part of the same process, to consumption.

To the extent that large-scale industry is developed, the creation of real wealth comes to depend less and less on the labour time and the quantum of labour employed compared with the power of the agents set in motion during that labour time, which in its turn – in its powerful effectiveness – is not minimally related to the immediate labour time that their production costs, but depends rather on the general state of science and of the progress of technology, or of the application of this science to production. ... Work no longer seems to be included in the production process as man rather stands apart

4. See Tom Nairn: *The Beginning of the End*, Panther Books, 1968, for a full development of this thesis. I have found Nairn's analysis most helpful.

from the production process as its regulator and guardian (what has been said of machines also applies to the combination of human activities and the development of human commerce).[5]

The computer is, so far, our most perfect expression of the fact that a machine performs man's work and he is only guardian over it. But in this occurrence, something inevitably happens to the man. No longer, as in early capitalism, is his work merely alienated in the seizure, by capital, of the object he creates, he, himself, is no longer an individual worker: he produces nothing, merely supervises what the machine produces. Scientific processes themselves increasingly regulate the reproduction and growth of wealth towards greater abundance, the work of the individual is dwarfed in power by the machine: only the greatly enlarged collective labour of man is of use to keep the process operating. The trained personnel come into their own: technicians of the production industry, the consumer industry, the media industry. The expansion of universities in England and America is to cater for this new demand for 'guardians' of the process of production, surveyors of that production's reproduction.

At the same time, there is, of course, an implicit contradiction. The late capitalist society that needs this educational expansion to provide its agents to develop the consciousness and hence the market, also overdoes it. It is not just that too many students (or drop-outs) are produced for the number of jobs available; it is that the very values inculcated by the education and by the jobs are liable to boomerang.

The Contradictions of Consumer Consciousness

A person's physical energies can be visibly harnessed and exploited. Buying mental energies is riskier. The very ideology that claims a 'man's thoughts are his own' and that all is free-choice (you can choose between one product and a thousand

5. Karl Marx: *Foundations for a Critique of Political Economy*, 1857–8. The section from which this is taken is translated by Ben Brewster as 'Marx's Notes on Machines' in *Sublation*, 1966, pp. 14–15.

others) serves to protect him. By an ironic twist the mental values we stimulate can be the death-knell of their own exploitation. Expanding the consciousness of many (for the sake of expanding consumerism) *does* mean expanding their consciousness. And the products of this expanded consciousness are more elusive than those of the factory conveyor belt. The ideologies cultivated in order to achieve ultimate control of the market (the free choice of the individual of whatever brand of car suits his individuality) are ones which can rebel *in their own terms*. The cult of the individual can surpass its use by the system to become that radical revolt of 'do-your-own-thing'. The cult of 'being true to your own feelings' becomes dangerous when those feelings are no longer ones that the society would like you to feel. Testing the quality of your world on your own pulse can bring about some pretty strange heart-beats. The media that enables you to *experience* the feelings of the world, brings the Vietcong guerrilla into your own living-room along with the whitest wash of all. The people who are supposed to 'manipulate' this expanded consciousness are only, in fact, its agents and they are thus quite likely to rebel within it.

The extension of consciousness of advanced capitalism (witnessed most easily in the growth of the communications industry) is the essential context for the form that nearly all radical politics took in the 1960s. That form echoes its context. The ideological revolution has initially, and predictably, taken the form of asserting the reality of the values that the old society pretends to elevate: individualism, subjectivity, personal freedom and choice, the soul.

Contradictions within the Ideological Institutions Themselves

Without a highly articulated, ramified ideological world, a consumer society could not exist. And if the educational institutions produce an ideology fraught with contradictions there is likely to be something contradictory within these

institutions themselves. The growth of ideology depends
upon the institutions which produce it: the educational and
socializing institutions. The schools, the colleges, the family:
in the home and at school, children are brought up to *believe*
in the world. This belief is not a faith: it is all the ideas and
expectations (or lack of both) that we have about the world,
themselves included. Since the end of the Second World War,
but yet more emphatically since the decline of the cold war,
there has been an ever-increasing stress on the role of the
family and of the school as centres for the production of
ideology. During a war, or even a 'cold war', coercion and
repression can be much more overt: the development of 'consensus' means the expansion of training, the 'internalizing'
of obedience; the encouragement of tolerance necessitates our
'instinctive' conformity. On the whole, schools and families
make quite a good job of it.

Yet as soon as this conformity recoils on itself, then the
institutions that have engendered it must be called into question. Women, Hippies, youth groups, students and school
children all question the institutions that have formed them,
and try to erect their obverse: a collective commune to replace
the bourgeois family; 'free communications' and counter-
media; anti-universities – all attack major ideological institutions of this society. The assaults are specified, localized
and relevant. They bring the contradictions out into the open.
This gives the movements staying power beyond the current
set-backs. For example, in challenging – often violently – the
institutions for the propagation of consensus, the students
have unleashed the powers of coercive state violence that are
always there as a background support. It is this inevitable
relationship between the quietude of consensus and the
brutality of coercion (the killings, beatings-up, imprison-
ments) that has shocked the intelligentsia and brought liberals
rallying round to preserve the university as an ivory-tower
enclave, isolated and immune from its own social function.
The conflict in the university is between its ideology of its own
privacy and 'free-speech' and its increasingly obvious public
functions, not just to provide the right economic workers but

to train personnel for the maintenance of the ideological structure itself; an ideological structure that radical students reject.

Class and Culture

The counter-cultural protests of the sixties, their most explicit exponents with the youth movement – Hippies, Yippies, students and school children – occupy different places in the spectrum of ideological revolutionaries. At their lowest, most unpolitical point, this revolt merely elevates the ideological qualities that current capitalist régimes claim to espouse but really abuse: selfhood and the free individual. This assertion of the possibility of realizing the temptations offered as sops by a capitalist society is a backward-looking Utopianism only too prone to reaction. At the other, and most political point, the onslaught on ideology attacks the institutions of its incarnation: the family, education and the media. It is inevitable that in almost all its manifestations this ideological or 'superstructural' revolution should be initiated by people of middle-class origin. By and large, only middle-class children go on to higher education (or stay at school beyond fifteen), or those that do continue their education, in this way become middle-class; working in the media is largely a middle-class job (conditions, salaries, expectations, etc.); it is middle-class children who can afford to 'drop out' and experiment with living styles; middle-class mothers who can contemplate the implications of the small nuclear family. But this is only the phenomenal form: more important than this is the fact that the dominant ideology of a capitalist society is the bourgeois one.

The class divisions that operate within the economic base apply within the superstructure, but not simply in a reflective manner. Each class has aspects of its own culture, which are relatively autonomous. This fact is illustrated by such phrases as 'working-class culture', 'ghetto-culture', 'immigrant-culture', etc. and by the absent phrase – 'middle-class culture'. We talk of middle-class mores: manners and habits (*U and non-U*) but not of a whole 'culture'. We don't think of 'middle-class culture' as something separate – it simply *is* the overall culture, within which are inserted these isolable other cultures. However, this cultural hegemony by bourgeois thought is not on an absolute par with the domination within the economy by the capitalist class. There is no sense in which one 'culture' can rise up and overthrow the one that dominates it. The mode of ideological domination is such as to make its domination invisible (its role, of course, is also to obscure the economic domination by its own class). Its aim – and achievement – is precisely to unify the otherwise opposing groups; to bury class antagonism beneath a welter of divergent, totally irrelevant alternatives (if it is a liberal democracy, tolerating 'free thought', a thousand sects – religious or political – obliterate *one* class), or beneath an homogenizing unity of purpose (e.g. the nationalism and racism of fascism, etc.). There is no cultural conflict because social groups remain fairly isolated from each other – in fact all the sub-cultures manage to establish are a series of communication barriers. It is not a case of one class operating the machinery of another class, but of one class being given breathing space for its own cultural habits within the total aerial environment of another class.

For this reason, among others, there is no chance of the working class rising up and simply asserting their cultural values over and against those of the middle class. The ideological dimensions of the revolution are likely *to come initially from within the ideologically dominant class*. Clearly nothing will be achieved within this sphere alone: nothing – even ideological – can be changed without a transformation of the economic base. So far all revolutions have occurred, and all classical Marxist analyses developed, in countries with early capitalist or feudal-capitalist systems. Although ideology is a permanent feature of all societies, the balance between it and the economy varies. In conditions of coercion and grotesque economic scarcity, it is not that the ideological weapons of oppression are diminished, but that the exploitation of the base is more visible. In a consumer society the role of ideology is so important that it is within the sphere of ideology that the oppressions of the whole system sometimes manifest themselves most apparently. It is here that middle-class radicalism has its place.

This should not mislead us into thinking that attacking the institutions and agents of the superstructure is a middle-class occupation and that, say, students must just ally with workers who will bring in the economic struggle. That would be a parody of the division of labour that capitalism offers us. The structure of advanced capitalism – both at home and in its imperialist actions in pre-capitalist countries – suggests that the role of *oppressed* groups, that is those groups which experience their oppression as much culturally as economically, is increasingly important. Women are an oppressed half of the population.

Background to the Women's Liberation Movement

The contemporary Women's Liberation Movement has been formed by a series of reactions – isolated within the Civil Rights Movement in the U.S.A., whites withdrew to student power and draft-resistance, isolated once more within these groups, women withdrew into Women's Liberation. Each withdrawal has strengthened that segment and as none of the movements from which each emerged has disintegrated with success (as in the nineteenth century, Abolition was won, or, in the early twentieth, the vote granted) so alliances with, or influence within, these other radical movements has become possible. Consequently, the revolutionary implications are greater. A complex attack on a system is likely to be stronger (politically rather than in actional terms) than a situation in which one political movement evolves from the ashes of another.

Although the recent chronological development ran from Blacks, students and Hippies to women, I think that the common context just described produced them all, enabling one movement to exist in a country in which another does not. This common context has been crucial in the formation of

Women's Liberation. It is this context which establishes a break with earlier feminism, and which establishes the struggle against oppression as a revolutionary one – a struggle in which all oppressed groups can ultimately be allied.

If the suffragettes as a whole in England had seen their battle (as a few did) as distinct from but comparable to that of the oppressed Irish (rebelling at the same time against colonialism), they could never have landed up handing out the white feather or calling their paper the *Britannia*. The most prominent of them never submerged their class interest in their own feminist struggle. Today, the conditions for doing precisely this are present.

The predominantly middle-class membership of the earlier feminist struggles *did* limit them: among other things, it directed them (despite the acute awareness by some members of working-class and/or Black problems) towards focussing on largely bourgeois issues. So Christabel Pankhurst could contend that even if the vote were given to red-haired women of a certain stature, their aims would have been achieved. And indeed, when in 1918 in England it was given to women over thirty who owned property, the most powerful wing of the movement was satisfied and the force of the struggle evaporated. Today, the issue cannot be so clear cut, nor the various issues subordinated to one legal, symbolic gesture. This is at least, in part, because of the changing nature of this type of middle-class movement.

Women and Education

It is far too crude to claim in an unqualified way that the Women's Liberation Movement is middle-class, but this is always done. Its largest membership comes from the 'educated' middle class and it arose in a country (the U.S.A.) where education is the ultimate aspiration, and where its availability is enormous and far more inclusive than in any previous epoch, and where women uniquely form forty-two per cent of college students. The changing implications of the educational system and the new jobs to which it is geared have crucially affected women. Other than as teachers, women have never been the traditional intellectuals – administrators, Members of Parliament, lawyers, clergy, etc. And now, educated, sans large families, apparently technocratized out of the home, these women move straight into new industrial jobs in a consumer society. Indeed it is the growth of these industries that may well, by a turn of the screw, have made possible the expansion in America of university places for women: women are particularly suitable for the glamorous lower reaches of the media industry as, apparently, they are suited for computer-programmers and jobs in comparable, less 'pure' reaches of science.[6]

The ideological manipulations and alienations of higher education affect women, as they affect all the other groups we have discussed. This is equally true of the industries responsible for the expansion of consumer-consciousness – advertising and the media. Though here women are presented with a further contradiction that male students as a whole escape. The jobs they are going into – which in any case are so far removed from their own production – tend, by a further twist, to use women as *their* means of reproduction. The woman working for the media, supervises the activities of the media, which themselves re-produce the product by means which, as often as not, are herself. It is hard to explain this Frankenstein nightmare. The machine has taken over production from man, and also ensures its own reproduction: its means of doing this is – among other things – to produce a constant market (a consumer market), the means of creating this is to sell a product – the means to sell a product is a sexy woman. The contortions of this process of alienation truly make an 'object' of the 'guardian' involved. It was inevitable that one of the first protests of the Women's Liberation Movement was against the use of women as 'sexual objects' in the whole communications industry.

6. As if to confirm this point, it is here, in the media, computer-programming, advertising, that, at least in intention, there is equal opportunity – it is in the older professions that overt discrimination prevails.

Women's Liberation and the Politics of Experience

The aspect of the ideological revolution that has enabled the
promotion of 'feelings' to the ranks of political action (the
'politics of experience', propagated above all by Hippies) has
certainly had important liberating effects: it has also opened up
political possibilities to completely new groups of people.
However, while being a crucial initiator of Women's Liberation itself, sometimes it has also boomeranged back in a way
that has been highly detrimental. In the ideology of capitalist
society *women* have always been the chief repository of feelings.
They are thus among the first to gain from the radical 'capture' of emotionality from capitalist ideology for political
protest movements. But the elevation of this quality ignores
its really oppressive side within our society. Emotions cannot
be 'free' or 'true' in isolation: they are dependent today on a
social base that imprisons and determines them. The liberation
of emotionality, as a transformation that apparently takes
place on its own (within the superstructure alone) is impossible. Indeed, the belief in its possibility is an ironic self-
parody. Late capitalist ideology precisely urges one to be free
in faith, personal and individual in emotions, and to think that
one can be this without a socio-economic transformation;
much Hippy ideology has merely explored this possibility.

Here, as with all the other radical movements in which they
initially participated, women have found their inspiration and
their desolation. The fight for Black rights, at first, seemed to
transcend sexual discrimination; the students were men and
women; the Hippy communes accorded women the newly
glorious role of emotionality and creativity.... But discrimination runs deep, oppression is larger than the sum total
of all these radical offerings. The economic changes that
thrust into revolutionary prominence the new 'educated',
youthful middle class, that provoked radical attacks on the
ideological institutions, caused the rise of the Women's
Liberation Movement. Once it had arisen, like its predecessor
Black Power, it saw that its tasks were greater than its origins:

that women's oppression manifests itself in economic and cultural deprivation, that oppressed women are found in all exploited minorities, in all social classes, in all radical movements. That on the issue of the position of women, friends are foes. It is with these realizations that the theory and practice of the movement has to contend.

Chapter Two

The Women's Liberation Movement

Discrimination Against Women: Preconditions of the Movement

Comparable conditions for women and comparable discriminations against them operate in all the countries where Liberation Movements have arisen. The similarity in the position of women in these countries may have relevance for the development of the movements there; indeed, it may be a precondition of their existence. These are industrial countries. Women's Liberation has not developed in rural areas, farming or peasant. In Italy, for example, it is mainly to be found in the cities of the North.

Outside the socialist countries these are the main nations in the world with egalitarian programmes: they are liberal democracies, ostensibly organized through consensus politics. Within the ideology of equality, the overt discriminatory practices come as a shock.[1] The egalitarian ideology does not mask a gap between the 'reality' and the 'illusion' offered but, on the contrary, is the way in which both the discrimination and the opposition to it is lived. The belief in the rightness and possibility of equality that women share has enabled them to feel 'cheated' and hence has acted as a precondition of their initial protest. In fact, what we are witnessing in this general denigration of women is an inevitable consequence of the socio-economic system of capitalism in which it operates. The inferiorization of women is essential to its functioning.

1. Or do they? Maybe the struggles of oppressed peoples in the advanced capitalist world with their constant expression of outrage at the abuses they suffer contribute to maintaining an equilibrium. The structural inequities and inegalities of capitalist society are made less visible by each assumption that they should not be there. Could these be as effectively concealed by revolutionary demands as they are by reformism?

Yet offered a mystifying emancipation and participating in an ideology of equality, the sense of something wrong is more acute than where women share in the openly dominative structures of feudal, semi-feudal or early capitalist societies.

All the countries characterized by Women's Liberation groups can point to the same areas and usually something like the same degrees of discrimination. Women in all the countries constitute a little more than one third of the labour force (the American figure of forty-two per cent is the highest). Their wages range from around half to nearly three quarters of the equivalent male wages. The largest percentages of women workers are, in all cases, in unskilled jobs. All countries in signing the Treaty of Rome, ratifying the International Labour Office agreement, or instigating their own Equal Pay Acts are committed (in slightly varying ways) to authorizing equal pay to all workers for equal work. In England it has been on the Trade Union Agenda since 1888.

Girls compose from less than one quarter to over one third of the university student body. The American figure is exceptional. In no other country are they more than twenty-six per cent. In nearly all cases, though they can leave school as well qualified, their opportunities for higher education and further training (apprenticeships) or part-time study (day-release) are less than half as good as the boys'. In the majority of these countries there has been an acclaimed policy of equal educational facilities for all for the best part of a hundred years.

Legal discrimination disguises itself as 'protective' legislation. All countries operate some legal prohibitions on the type, hours and place of work of women and minors. The interests of the married woman are ostensibly safeguarded by the necessity of her maintenance during and after marriage. Usually her earnings are classified as part of her husband's income and the man, as assumed provider, is also legal custodian of the child. All these laws are the consequence of the woman's assumed dependence on the man – in fact, of course, they create and ensure it. This in countries which utilize women in what are recognized as the most exhausting jobs;

countries which do not simply extol motherhood, but more invidiously stress the profound implications of mother-love and nurturance: giving her the tasks and him the rights.

Degrees of availability of contraception and abortion differ in the various countries. In all of them its distribution and safety is random and haphazard. In none of them is it considered the automatic right of every woman. In all of them it is the privilege of the rich (white middle class) or the abuse of the poor (e.g. the use of Puerto Ricans as guinea pigs in testing birth control devices). Even the most liberal laws on abortion, as in Scandinavia, England and New York, force the woman to provide 'reasons' which are equivalent to self-denigration (physical or financial difficulties are rarely as acceptable as confession of psychological ineptitude). All this in industrial countries urging (for the rest of the world?) population control: countries extolling individualism and its correlate – a high degree of personal attention for the young child.

All these countries exhibit an essential imbalance of production and consumption. Women as housewives are seen as the main agents of consumption. The ethic of consumption (spending money) is counterposed divisively to that of production (creating wealth) – the province of the husband. Appealed to as consumers, women are also the chief agents of that appeal: used aesthetically and sexually they sell themselves to themselves. Used in these advertisements they also lure men into the temptation of 'luxury' spending. Woman's fundamental job as provider of food, health and welfare comes to seem an extravagance and so does she along with it. Her responsibility for the most basic needs of people is converted into a leisure-time activity and she a play-thing (if she is young enough) that accompanies such work. Both she and the job are evaluated accordingly. Despite her work, she represents leisure and sexuality. And this in industrial societies which have, at least in the Germanic, Anglo-Saxon and Scandanavian countries, an ethic of puritanism and hard work.

The Organization of the Movement

Women in the different countries experience a comparable oppression and the Women's Liberation Movements have comparable aims, but organizationally, and hence to some extent theoretically, they can be quite dissimilar. This diversity is largely due to their different origins. In England the length and strength of unionized working-class struggle is crucial, in Italy it is the Marxist students and in America the Black Power struggle. I have selected five countries, each with somewhat different problems and different methods of organizing. I hope thereby, to illustrate the diversity possible within a united aim: the Liberation of Women.

England

The first whisperings of the Women's Liberation Movement in England were late in 1967; by 1968 it was a named and organized movement. Its earliest manifestations were from three distinct sources: American radical politics, psycho-cultural-political groups and, in 1968, the labour movement. Specifically these were the American women in London working against the Vietnam war and for U.S. deserters (e.g. The Stoppit Committee), the grass-roots politics of Agitprop and the psycho-politics of the Dialectics of Liberation Congress and the Anti-University, and then the strike of Ford women workers for equal pay. Later these seminal groups were joined by women discontented with their role in the Revolutionary Socialist Students Federation, and first caucuses and then separate groups were formed within the traditional left sects. Many already existent equal-rights organizations quickly identified or provided an overlapping membership – for instance, the Open Door International and Mothers in Action. By late 1969 many of the major towns had Women's Liberation groups and a number of the larger cities, particularly London, had several different organizations in operation. The basic principle of organization is the small group (see pp. 59–60). In March, 1970, the first national conference took place. Originally called by a group of women historians as a small study workshop, it was transformed by the growing urgency of the disparate groups and of individual women into a week-end conference of 600 participants. The present organization of the Women's Liberation Movement in Britain stems from the resolutions of this conference.

The conference set up a National Co-ordinating Committee (N.C.C.) composed of two representatives from each group (this composition is, in fact, fairly informal except for voting on controversial issues). It is an umbrella organization without initiatory powers and without a programme. Any group can ask for support from other groups for its campaigns and actions; only if all participant groups agree does it become the responsibility of the N.C.C. – for instance, as in the case of the nationwide demonstrations on International Women's Day, 6–8 March (1971). The N.C.C. is entrusted with the setting up of national conferences to be held three or four times a year in different regions (so far in Oxford, Sheffield, Liverpool). Of course, in a new movement forging new theory there is a wide political spectrum – from Liberal-radical through to revolutionary socialist and anarchist, with all the different tendencies within each. Sectarian differences are present, and are the joy of an antagonistic media. When the media first latched on to Women's Liberation, the divisive tactic was to set Liberationist women arguing against women who opposed the movement. Now that the commercial instinct has hailed 1971 as the year of the feminists, the divisive strategy is more sycophantic: set different groups of the Women's Liberation Movement to argue against each other, or say where they differ. As a result of a bad experience of this sort, the N.C.C. made one of its regulations that each group could describe their own politics to the press, etc. but not those of other groups. The hope is to keep disagreement for fruitful debate within the movement and to prevent the sectarian battles that have riddled so many previous revolutionary movements. There is all the difference in the world between the proliferation of different autonomous groups and divisive fragmentation.

Because the groups are autonomous one cannot describe a united political aim; however, the very existence of a national organization presupposes some shared assumptions. Women's Liberation in England is a broad-based movement, hence, it is primarily concerned with all women, no matter what their political experience or opinion. For some, the grass-roots concept is in itself the correct one, for others the more ortho-dox Marxist conception of a small formation of revolutionary cadres may be on the agenda – understandably, in the absence of a Marxist analysis of women's oppression, its time is being postponed. Most, but not all, of the English groups are closed to men.

Holland[2]

Holland is in many respects a comparable country to England. Ostensibly, it is highly 'democratic' and tolerant, in the first instance, of protest and non-conformity. One of the strands in the political life of the sixties that was important for the de-velopment of the Women's Liberation Movement in England was yet more crucial in Holland – the anarcho-culturalist protest movement. The Provos, whose demonstrations pro-voked the state violence behind the velvet glove of 'con-sensus' democracy, gave way in the late sixties to groups who mocked and teased the institutions they wanted to destroy. It is within this tradition that one of Holland's two large Women's Liberation groups exists – the Dolle Minas. Their actions are playful and offensive – thereby illustrating the underlying insult behind the 'normal' treatment of women: they wolf-whistle and pinch men's bottoms, tie pink ribbons round urinals, considerably discomposing the staid Dutch burgher. Many of the women joined a women's movement through dissatisfaction with their 'feminine' roles in student and other

2. See Margaret Walter's description in *Shrew*, November–December, 1970. I am totally indebted to her for this section on Holland, which, to all intents and purposes, is a 'quotation' of her article.

radical groups. It is interesting that though there are many
Marxists among the Dolle Minas, their orientation (reflecting
their heritage mentioned above) seems to be largely cultural,
protesting sexual discrimination against women. The other
group MVM – Men and Women in Society – is larger, older
and 'serious-minded'. It concerns itself with the general
conditions of women within the already available social framework – with legal reform, with child-care facilities, with social
and economic discrimination. Its character and aims are comparable to those of the American National Organization of
Women.

The two groups seem very different; but despite this, and
despite their different origins, seen from a negative perspective
they are very alike. A lack of politics unites them. The former
group is culturalist, the latter reformist-economist and,
though both cultural and economic questions are together
crucial for political struggle, neither group seems to be over
concerned with making the connection. Perhaps symptomatic
of this – and certainly illustrative of a similarity that overrides
the apparent differences – is the fact that both groups are for
men and women, and men are frequently dominant.

Sweden

The experience of women in Sweden, throughout the last
decades has been somewhat different from that of women in
the other advanced capitalist countries. Sweden has always had
sexual egalitarianism high on its programme. Presenting itself
as the most democratic, nay, 'socialistic' of capitalist countries,
the emancipation of women has always been a good advertisement for the humanitarian fairness of its society. It
never fell into the glaring pitfalls that England sunk into in its
crude utilization of women for the economy where at one
moment women were 'manning' the munitions factories, the
next extolled as the housebound doll and mother. In Sweden
in the thirties, a commission headed by Alva Myrdal investigating the declining birthrate, recommended not that women
should be sent home to gestate and nurture, but that the state

should provide child-care facilities, flexible work hours and social amenities – family restaurants, laundries, communal housing, etc. Swedish women earn on average just over 70 per cent of a man's wage, jobs are officially open to all, education is the same for both sexes with boys learning household and child-care subjects. Contraception, abortion and divorce are relatively easy, the unmarried mother is not discriminated against. Countries unable to cope with such egalitarianism have made the usual conversion of tolerance into neurosis, fabricating for Sweden a phenomenal suicide rate and total promiscuity.

Yet this unabating concern with the position of women has also had its peak-moments and its tailing-off periods. Feminists rightly point out that discussions of the position of women are prominent in the news for those years when some important economic readjustment has to take place: for example, when there is a shortage of 'man-power', when more scientists, technicians, etc., are needed – as now. In other countries the actual *position* of women is, of course, also crucially affected by different economic demands: in England, for instance, more teachers were wanted in the early sixties – hence it was suddenly discovered that married women had 'two lives' and could go back to such work after child-raising. Today, more engineers are wanted and women are suddenly declared suitable. But in Sweden this alteration is accompanied by a resurgence of explicit discussion (claiming to be disinterested) of women's roles. This overt debate can, in fact, *obscure* the issue: the economic expediency becomes invisible, behind the social concern. Indeed this problem is more generalizable. The very stress that Swedish society puts on sexual equality makes it hard to see the oppression of women. Until fairly recently this could be said to have had, inevitably, a retarding effect on a Women's Liberation Movement. Every demand that feminists made was readily incorporated: communes are well financed (privately or by government aid), a proposal for a working week of thirty hours for men and women was welcomed (whether it would ever have been instituted nationally is another matter) by big industrialists, at the time anxious to

decrease the work force without creating visible unemployment, a suggestion for paying housewives was supported by
conservatives (after all it *is* a way of keeping women at home).
In all countries where Women's Liberation groups occur there
are those who stress that their movement is for the liberation
of men and women (the creation of so-called 'whole people'):
only in Sweden was this notion institutionalized; in the mid-
sixties the 'women question' was renamed 'the sex-role
debate' – the ideology of equality had penetrated even a
movement that was set up to demonstrate its absence. Men
were as active as women, for the question was not the oppression of the one group but the relationship (individual and
generic) between the sexes.

However, by the late sixties the easy accommodation of the
problem was itself seen as problematic and groups specifically
for the Liberation of Women were established in Lund and
Stockholm. These tend to be explicitly Marxist groups and
seem to be following a Marxist model for organization. They
are not interested in forming a huge movement as yet (indeed
the success in terms of rapidly growing numbers is a problem)
but instead feel that the political and theoretical work has to
keep pace with numerical expansion. The development of a
'politics' which could keep command of a movement is
promulgated in two ways: through Marxist study groups and
through organizational work among women workers in low-
pay factories. The direction, then, has been from the wider,
inclusive discussion of 'sex-roles' to tighter Marxist groupings, analysing and organizing around women.

France

France presents an almost opposite phenomenon. Women's
Liberation started as a small group of Marxist women in Paris
in late 1968. Some were Americans, others mainly students
who had been active in the May Revolution. For over a year
they concentrated on Marxist theory, not attempting to grow
at all in numbers. Then they undertook the first action – a
demonstration at Vincennes University – the 'red ghetto'.

The vulgar (politically and sexually) reaction of their fellow male revolutionaries was extreme (see p. 86). Just previously representatives had attended the first English National Conference (Oxford, March, 1970). The two events – the attitudes of male 'comrades' and the broad base of the English movement – determined the Paris groups to open up. There are now a considerable number of neighbourhood groups both in Paris and in some provincial cities and there are sectarian Women's Liberation groups. The actions of all groups are militant and their position explicitly anti-capitalist; they attack the family and all laws that maintain it (the prohibition of abortion, for instance), they work on radicalizing concepts of child-rearing, they attack the commercial use of women by the media and they stress the oppression and exploitation of working-class women. There have always been close links between the French and English Women's Liberation groups and now, from very different beginnings and the somewhat different cultural and economic treatment of women in the two countries, the two movements bear closer and closer resemblances. The French groups have always been more explicitly socialist, usually Marxist, but from their Marxist notion of a cadre-formation they have moved, at the moment, to a broader-based movement. In England, the broad-based, all-inclusive movement has, I think, been growing more explicitly socialist (certainly more revolutionary) since its analyses have constantly come up against the bed-rock of oppression in a capitalist society. Though this strong leftwards tendency is, in turn, provoking some internal criticism.

The U.S.A.

I find it extremely difficult to write about the American Movement. Like America itself it seems to defy coherent analysis. One feels the movement is everywhere – but can often find it nowhere clearly. There are so many groups and so many different positions that it seems pointless to catalogue them here; it would be better to take up later some of the basic, shared concepts.

There is a further difficulty. In my other brief surveys I have relied on a combination of my own experience of the countries concerned and their movements, together with the analyses made by participant sisters. This is impossible with the American movement. An individual and a foreigner feels small both in relation to the size of the country and to the size of the movement. I have visited parts of the East Coast and the Mid-West but not the South or the West Coast. I have held discussions with many groups and individuals – but an overview cannot come from this. In America, you talk with people to find out the perspectives of their group, what they are doing and where they see themselves as differing from other groups. This is not equivalent to the sectarian differences found, say, in England – differences of political analysis that pre-date the Women's Liberation Movement; on the contrary, it is intrinsic to the growth of Women's Liberation itself. The formation of different groups with diverse political analyses is *how* the movement and *how* the analyses of women's oppression develop in America. This is true of nowhere else – not even of neighbouring Canada. Nor, interestingly, is it true of the Student or Peace (in Vietnam) Movement. It is true, somewhat differently, of the Black Movement.

The Black Movement was probably the greatest single inspiration to the growth of Women's Liberation. It started with the relatively moderate beginnings of the Civil Rights protest in the early sixties, and at each encounter with the hostile racist society, grew more militant. The progress of Black Power has been from a broad, open opposition movement to a successively narrowing and intensifying revolutionary-cadre organization. In the process of developing revolutionary concentration a number of militant groups were formed, of which the Black Panthers are the best known. Something roughly comparable happened with Women's Liberation; it moved from a broad-based egalitarian, oppositionist struggle (now seen as reformist – even more chronically so than Martin Luther King among the Blacks) to a number of organizationally tighter and analytically and practically more revolutionary groups – to a political position of radical feminism:

Radical feminism recognizes the oppression of women as a fundamental political oppression wherein women are categorized as an inferior class based upon their sex. It is the aim of radical feminism to organize politically to destroy this sex class system. As radical feminists we recognize that we are engaged in a power struggle with men, and that the agent of our oppression is man in so far as he identifies with and carries out the supremacy privileges of the male role. For while we realize that the liberation of women will ultimately mean the liberation of men from the destructive role as oppressor, we have no illusion that men will welcome this liberation without a struggle.... Radical feminism is political because it recognizes that a group of individuals (men) have set up institutions throughout society to maintain this power.[3]

Much as, roughly speaking, the central heritage of the Black Movement progressed from Civil Rights through Black Muslims to Black Panthers; so the Women's Liberation Movement has moved from reformist (NOW) through liberationists to radical feminists. Each development of the movement is in some sense a progressive departure from earlier positions, yet it is important that in the Women's Liberation Movement they continue to co-exist. The main reformist group – the National Organization of Women which originated the struggle in 1967 is still, by a long way, the largest single group, highly organized and very active. The distinction between Liberationist and Radical Feminist doesn't exist in Europe (nor in large parts of America); I discuss its meaning later (pp. 65–6), but for most of this book I have used the term 'feminist' and 'liberationist' somewhat interchangeably and refer to the whole movement as the Women's Liberation Movement. Briefly, liberationists see the oppression of women as one (though a major one) of the many oppressions experienced by different people in pre-socialist societies; radical feminists contend it is the major and primary one in all societies.

This distinction between radical feminists and liberationists first found expression as a division between feminists and so-called 'politicos'. The latter were those women who still

3. 'New York Radical Feminist Manifesto', quoted Cellestine Ware: *Woman Power,* Tower Public Affairs Books, 1970, pp. 58.

worked in alliance with other revolutionary activities – protesting against the Vietnamese war, aiding draft resistance, etc. – and whose analysis was that women were a crucial part of the revolutionary struggle against capitalism. For radical feminists, as the oppression of women is the primary oppression in all societies, whatever their mode of production, a revolution here is the priority – from this all the other changes would follow. However, this division seems now somewhat less important. Maybe this is due to the recession of other highly vocal radical activity in the States (the decimation of the Panthers, the retreat of 'Weathermen', the ageing of the Yippies, the uncertainties of the Vietnam Peace Movement) and to the prominence of Women's Liberation in the vanguard of revolutionary action.

If a single inspiration for the movement is to be cited, it was the publication in 1963 of Betty Friedan's *The Feminine Mystique*[4] (and her subsequent foundation of NOW in 1966). More interesting, however, is the larger political source of the movement. Broadly, it seems to have come together from three directions. The discontent of middle-class, often middle-aged, women who, told that they lived in a matriarchal society (they dominated their kids with 'momism', owned most of the wealth, got their husbands to the kitchen sink and doing the diaper wash), nevertheless found themselves unable to get professional jobs or rise anywhere on the vocational ladder. A second source was the dissatisfaction of white women militants with their treatment in the Civil Rights Movement and within Students for a Democratic Society; in both, they were 'typists, tea-makers and sexual objects'. A third was the counter-culture, 'politics of experience', and new political sensibility that produced so many different groups in the mid-sixties.

The Women's Liberation Movement in America differed from the later movements in the other countries in not having either a labour movement as one of its component influences, nor, at its inception, a socialist stress on the working-class as the revolutionary class. The socialist women in the movement

4. Betty Friedan: *The Feminine Mystique*, New York, 1963.

were mainly students, in a country seen to be cut up more along ethnic than class lines. The movement, as elsewhere, was mainly white and so-called middle-class – this provoked a double anxiety where in the European countries there is only one: in 1968, the absence of black women in the movement, in 1969, the absence of working-class women.

The absence of Black women has provoked a changing awareness. Initially, the importance of the concept of Black Power was so crucial to the analysis of the situation of women, that Black women's involvement and support was constantly sought. After all, the Black assertion of themselves as an oppressed people within the homeland of imperialist-capitalism led to a comparable realization about women. Both struggles are against oppression in the 'First World'. But a crucial difference led to further definition. Where Black Americans are massively economically exploited and can thus afford to omit their tiny Black bourgeoisie from the revolutionary struggle, women's oppression does not coincide so simply with the lowest economic groups: all women, whatever their class, are oppressed *as women*. However, for Black women not to be involved in the Women's Liberation Movement was critical as it seemed like a competition rather than an alliance between oppressed groups. Analysis then showed that the wage-structure of American society showed the following order: white men, black men, white women, black women. At work, black men did marginally better than white women. Black women were the most oppressed and exploited people within the whole society and, in addition, were often oppressed within their own Black Power Movement: Black men were to be powerful, Black women pregnant. But a coming together of the analysis of the omnipresent oppression of women, by most revolutionary women within both movements (Women's Liberation and Black Power) seems, currently, to be overcoming the earlier divisive situation. There are now black women in their own groups and in the pre-existent Women's Liberation groups, and working-class women are joining in ever increasing numbers as the movement spreads into the factories.

Some of the Women's Liberation groups are highly organized, with conditions of membership, regular literature, planned campaigns and constant analysis; others are often informal 'consciousness-raising' groups (see p. 61–63). In many of the cities, different groups have come together to set up a centre which provides information about the movement, advice on contraception and abortion, child-care, etc., literature on the status of women and a political focal point.

Thus we see a heterogeneous movement with numerous successes, a proliferating literature, an already visible change in the sensibilities and attitudes of many people to women, and – perhaps most triumphantly – its own size and growth to its credit. Women are uniting.

The Campaigns, Organization and Concepts of Women's Liberation – So Far

Behind and around Women's Liberation, can be seen the entire youth culture and the political groupings of the sixties – Hippies, Yippies and others. There is Civil Rights and the Black Power Movement, organized student militancy, anarchism, and anarcho-terrorism and left-wing terrorism, sectarian groups, and reformist 'Equal Rights' groups that have all had a reflorescence in the name of Women's Liberation. The psycho-politics of experience, the regroupings of the New Left and, in England at least, some increase in Trade Union dynamism have all influenced the formation of Women's Liberation and been influenced by it.

Like most of these political movements, Women's Liberation started with a series of complaints – complaints against the society and against the radical groups that were supposed to be challenging this. In forming itself one of its earliest tasks was to transform these complaints into (a) a political challenge to the social institutions, and (b) to develop an organization that in its form and content would eradicate the relevant faults of the other preceding radical groups.

Campaigns and Their Implications

In all the countries concerned, the Women's Liberation Movement has launched campaigns aimed at all the major dimensions of women's oppression: economic, legal and sexual;
her role in reproduction and the socializing of children. In
England, the national campaigns directly reflect this preoccupation with 'all fronts'. There is a nation-wide campaign
for equal pay, equal work and equal opportunities; for free
birth-control and abortion on demand; for a re-examination
of the whole educational set-up and for after-school children's
centres; for the provision of easily available, free pre-school
crèches and nurseries. Particular groups attack the ideological
exploitation of women as 'sexual objects' – by the media and
industrial enterprises based on this sexual exploitation, the
Playboy Club and Mecca's 'Miss World', for instance. The
national campaigns have many aspects. The promotion of
birth-control involves investigations of the attitudes of doctors and of women, the capricious, profit-oriented control of it
by chemical and rubber manufacturers, the arbitrariness of research into it and into allied gynaecological fields, the lack of
interest of the government, and the biased hyper-interest of
the press. The provision of nursery schools involves discussion
and analysis of the mother-child relationship from the view-
point of psychology – and of the mother concerned. The
sexual exploitation of women and their enforced submission
within a society committed – when it feels like it – to the
'naturalness' of their reproductive role, has caused the movement to develop the notion of the 'control of one's body'.
This slogan finds its meaning somewhere between 'having
control of one's own thoughts' (i.e. freedom of mind) and
'workers' control' (worker-run factories). Women do literally
sell their bodies – if not as prostitutes, then to the publicity
industries, modelling and so on – much as men and women
sell their labour power. As a worker finds himself alienated in
his own product, so (roughly speaking) a woman finds herself
alienated in her own commercialized body. The female body

in the advertisement may not be her own, but it *does* represent it. The mass of workers experience their alienation individually but women, in this way, experience it generically. The slogan protests against this as it protests against the other dimension: her submission to the arbitrariness of conception.

These are just some of the implications behind the major declared aims of, for instance, the English movement. If nothing else, they show how far reaching 'reform' can be where women's oppression is concerned. In America there are much more extensive campaigns: to reassess (and revalidate) the role of women in history, to eliminate sexism from the law, from the press and from school text-books (this is also happening in European countries – in fact, it was initiated in Sweden). Women in all countries are forming their own feminist theatre, their own pop-groups, their own cinema.

Principles of Organization

(1) Why just Women?

Many people, inside and outside the movement, argue that the liberation of women involves the liberation of men. Many people contend that the movement will get nowhere unless it can convince men, or at least explain to them, its importance. How can one sex be free without the other? Both sexes are oppressed by sex-role stereotypes ... don't you think men would like to be more at home with their children ... ? don't you think they would like not to have to go down the coal mines and be the breadwinners ... ? feminist women remember your womanly hearts and pity the woes of the oppressor ... socialist liberationist women remember that under capitalism *all* but the bourgeoisie suffer the slings and arrows of outrageous fortune.... Women of the world unite, no longer behind your men, but in front, be our vanguard, take the blows, forge the track, give us our revolution ...

In an effort to repudiate the days of obscene ridicule of Women's Liberation (see pp. 84–86), radical men who endorse the movement have taken up various postures in relation to it, ranging from the tilting, half-begging posture 'let us in' to the falling over backwards 'go ahead, show us the way, you're the new revolutionary hope ... we'll support you.'

At this stage, it feels strange to have to 'justify' an all-women movement – but as it still does disturb a lot of people and as some Women's Liberation groups have men members – it seems a good idea to try. It is hard to recall the reasons we first gave, the fear and embarassment we felt. Yet I do remember being surprised that it was 'all right' talking just to women. Many of us came out of predominantly male political movements, girl-friends belonged to childhood, women's coffee parties were not for us ... seriousness was men. I can remember a male comrade asking me who I'd lunched with and when I mentioned a woman's name, saying "I hate women who have other women for friends.' I can remember the men I worked with at my job and the men I worked with politically, saying complacently of me, 'Oh, she likes being the only woman. ...' I suppose my constant requests for more women were mere bluff. ... How could I not have been flattered by my position? And I suppose I was. What else was there to be? As women, could we afford to like each other without trivializing ourselves? So, at least in England, where Women's Liberation first started as an all-women movement, we said: 'Well, you see, women are shy in front of men, men do all the talking, take the dominant roles: women have got to learn to be active, to have confidence ... then, maybe, we can afford to let men in.' Today, I think, such defensiveness is only used tactically – to make someone really remote from the Movement view this aspect with (patronizing) sympathy and hence open him (or more importantly her) to other dimensions. Though that is not to say that it isn't still true – we still often defer (intellectually and/or flirtatiously) to men – it's just that the reason for segregation has got so obvious that we forget the excuses. It's simply that we are (in this case) the oppressed people and around this we organize.

The American Movement from its outset had the separatist analogy of Black Power; they never had to be quite so polite as we were – American women suffer less from the pedestal discrimination and the double-binds of old-world courtesy that afflict European women.

The separatist politics of Women's Liberation may have come out of one of the chief manifestations of women's oppression: their diffidence: but it certainly debouches straight into its central theory – that it is women as a group that are oppressed, and that, though all oppressed groups should work to a point of solidarity with each other, their own understanding of their own situation comes from their own analysis. As a militant women's organization, Women's Liberation both counteracts the oppressed behaviour of women in our society (women cannot be submissive, fragile, dependent, etc.), and provides a political base for the analysis of this oppression. Such a separatist movement in no way excludes the awareness of other oppressed groups under capitalism, nor does it pretend that the society does not harm men, too. The movement is largely anti-capitalist and as such assumes the distortion of everybody's life and potential today. But such generalities are moral, not political, and though everyone wants liberation for *all* (men and women) this cannot but be Utopianism unless at this stage, we organize around specific oppressions.

(2) Domination versus Collectivity

Opposing any form of domination in theory, and having suffered its effects in previous radical groups, all Women's Liberation politics act on the basis of developing collective work and preventing the rise of ego-tripping leaders. Outsiders, trying to pin down the politics of a group, complain of the lack of a centre. They are so used to 'spokesmen' that their absence confuses.

Women, having been trained and socialized to passivity and demureness, are particularly vulnerable to any offer to take a back seat once more. Many groups rotate organizational positions, interviews with the press, radio and television, speaking engagements, etc., so that no one develops a too powerful expertise and no one confirms her own inhibitions. Some groups, not wanting too great a diffuseness to result from the absence of a leader, structure their groups on a formal democratic basis: even making sure by institutional methods that no one shall either dominate or not participate in the time allotted for discussions. Other groups aim at writing papers or books collectively and at undertaking public speaking always in groups. This stress on collective work countermands both the hierarchic nature of the oppressive society and the isolation and/or subservience that women are forced into within the home and in their personal relationships.

Women, directed from childhood towards marriage, living in a 'man's world', relate primarily to men and mainly competitively with each other – whether for a man or for the cleanest wash in the neighbourhood. Working together with other women in a united struggle overcomes this isolation and competitiveness – collective work is part of the process; refusal of leaders is a refusal of male-female or competitive female-female relationships, such as they are in the society that is being challenged.

(3) The Small Group

The basic unit of organization in the Women's Liberation Movement is the small group of anything from six to two dozen women. As the group develops it transforms its nature. At first it is the means of bringing women into close personal solidarity and friendship with each other. In the final stage, many small groups see themselves as revolutionary collectives, whose task is to analyse the nature of women's oppression and thereby work out a strategy. The transition marks the changing awareness that as women's problems are not private and personal, so, neither is their solution; or, to put it another way, it reflects the change from personal self-awareness (in the psycho-therapeutic sense) to group-consciousness or the oppressed person's equivalent to 'class-consciousness'. The small group permits the transition from the personal to the political and simultaneously interrelates them. For women are socialized to two obverse reactions: either, because they are 'women', they can go on endlessly about their personal lives, or, because they are dominated by men, when they join a political organization, they imitate men's styles and cannot discuss the personal, but only analyse the so-called 'objective' situation which normally means, quite simply, somebody-else's problems somewhere else.

Women who cannot deal with the peculiar forms oppression takes in their private lives are highly suspect when they begin to talk about forms of oppression that afflict other women. The peculiarities and severity of oppression vary according to class and race and women of different classes and races must first deal with the particular forms of oppression found in their own situations. If we cannot face our own problems we have no right to claim that we have answers to other people's problems.[5]

The small group ensures that each individual is safe enough (through solidarity and non-judgement) to probe the experience of personal oppression (to howl and shout, cry and complain) and on this basis to understand others and how oppression comes about.

Concepts of Women's Liberation

The political organization of Women's Liberation as an all-women movement based on maximum collective work and minimum domination by 'leaders' has produced (and has itself been produced by) certain concepts. These concepts are, on the one hand, its initial contribution to the development of its new politics, or, on the other, an expression of the understanding of the oppression of women. Into the first category comes 'consciousness-raising', and 'no leaders' and 'non-élitism'; into the second comes 'sexism', 'male chauvinism' and 'feminism'. In either borrowing or originating these concepts, Women's Liberation makes the first move towards transcending its own beginnings (the first 'complaints' that

5. Pamela Allen: *The Small Group Process*, San Francisco Women's Liberation, p. 15. in *The Small Group, Three Articles by Lynn O'Connor, Pam Allen, Liz Bunding*, Women's Liberation Basement Press, Berkeley.

women made) and towards organizing itself as a political
movement.

(1) Consciousness-Raising

Many liberationists see consciousness-raising as one of the
most important contributions of the movement to a new
politics. Women's Liberation is crucially concerned with that
area of politics which is experienced as personal. Women
come into the movement from the unspecified frustration of
their own private lives, find that what they thought was an
individual dilemma is a social predicament and hence a political
problem. The process of transforming the hidden, individual
fears of women into a shared awareness of the meaning of
them as social problems, the release of anger, anxiety, the
struggle of proclaiming the painful and transforming it into
the political – this process is *consciousness-raising*. A paradigm
that is often given is of a small group of women one of whom
decides to describe all her feelings connected with an abortion
she has had; in turn, people follow suit. If they haven't had
abortions, then their fears, social-moral attitudes, etc. In this
way a personal incident that was condemned to the oblivion of
privacy is examined as a manifestation of the oppressed conditions women experience: the personal is seen to be a crucial
aspect of the political.

Detractors deride consciousness-raising sessions as 'group
therapy'. The accusation is more interesting than it is meant
to be. It reveals both inaccuracy and prejudice. One might well
ask why, in a country like the United States, with a middle-
class urban population that is virtually besotted with the need
for psycho-therapy and psychiatry, there is (a) anything wrong
with people imitating 'group therapy' and (b) why they don't
know what group therapy is? In a Women's Liberation
consciousness-raising session there is, quite simply, no 'impar-
tial' therapist: all are involved and at stake. But why, if it were
the case, would it be a slur? Of course, the apparent denigration
of therapy is really only a concealed put-down of women: oh,
they're moaning again, gossiping their complaints, having a

nag ... what they need is a good therapist (twentieth-century
parent-surrogate punisher).

In fact, the concept of 'consciousness-raising' is the reinterpretation of a Chinese revolutionary practice of 'speaking
bitterness' – a reinterpretation made by middle-class women in
place of Chinese peasants and in a country riddled by psycho-
therapeutic practices. These peasants, subdued by violent
coercion and abject poverty, took a step out of thinking their
fate was natural by articulating it. The first symptom of oppression is the repression of words; the state of suffering is so
total and so assumed that it is not known to be there. 'Speaking
bitterness' is the bringing to consciousness of the virtually
unconscious oppression; one person's realization of an in-
justice brings to mind other injustices for the whole group.
Nobody suggests that this revolutionary practice could be
imported wholesale from the conditions of peasants in pre-
revolutionary China to Women's Liberation Movements in
the advanced capitalist countries. But there is a relevance
which doesn't insult the plight of the Chinese peasant. In
having been given for so long their own sphere, their 'other'
world, women's oppression is hidden far from consciousness
(this dilemma is expressed as 'women don't want liberating');
it is this acceptance of a situation as 'natural', or a misery as
'personal' that has first to be overcome. 'Consciousness-
raising' is speaking the unspoken: the opposite, in fact, of
'nattering together'.

Speaking the unspoken is, of course, also the purpose of
serious psychoanalytic work. Unfortunately, it is not the prevalent purpose. The concept and practice of 'consciousness-
raising' *has* suffered a debasement by its development in a
country sold over to debased psychotherapy. The spread of the
Esselin methods and of 'encounter-therapy' has had its effects
on many aspects of radical politics. Ostensibly evoking the
unspoken (more normally the 'unspeakable' in its restricted
sense), provoking the unholy (enforcing taboo – sensual, sexual and soulful 'touching' between 'untouchable' strangers),
this 'therapy' has taught us the scope of our inhibitions – but
only for the sake of it. Brought up in a society that inhibits us,

as inhibited individuals we go to an encounter-therapy session to meet other inhibited individuals. We break our inhibitions, 'make contact' and . . . become uninhibited individuals? Maybe – for what? Do we thus gain inner peace, strength, 'togetherness'? For what? From inhibited individual, through the group, to the uninhibited individual. The circles of the mind. Revolutionary politics is linear – it must move from the individual, to the small group, to the whole society.

Some of the Women's Liberation 'consciousness-raising' groups have suffered the fate of the whirlpool. Individual – small group – individual. Lonely women have left home and gone back home. Never moving out of the small circle, the fervour of the Chinese peasant has become the fashion of the middle-class American. Women's Liberation knows this, as it knows that the ability to articulate is a privilege that is easily abused:

Women in the group also felt that consciousness-raising should be a means to the development of a politics and not as an end in itself. Women in the group also felt that consciousness-raising was particularly suited to the highly articulate women of the middle and upper classes and that these women were able to gain ascendency over the group through their proficiency in this central activity of the Group.[6]

(2) Male Chauvinism and Male Supremacy

'Male chauvinism' is being too much of a man. Either the male chauvinist has internalized the domination of men within our society and, in his individual actions and attitudes epitomizes this 'supremacy' or, as radical feminists believe, this attitude pre-exists any specific social formation:

. . . We believe that the purpose of male chauvinism is primarily to obtain psychological ego satisfaction, and that only secondarily does this manifest itself in economic relationships. . . . For this reason we do not believe that capitalism, or any other economic system, is the cause of female oppression, nor do we believe that female oppression will disappear as a result of a purely economic

6. Pamela Allen: op. cit., p. 12.

revolution. The political oppression of women has its own class dynamic. And that dynamic must be understood in terms previously called 'non-political' – namely the politics of the ego . . . the male ego identity (is) sustained through its ability to have power over the female ego. Man establishes his 'manhood' in direct proportion to his ability to have his ego override hers, and derives his strength and self-esteem through this process. This male need, though destructive, is in that sense, impersonal. It is not out of a desire to hurt the woman that he dominates her and destroys her; it is out of a need for a sense of power that he necessarily must destroy her ego and make it subservient to his . . .[7]

The radical feminists postulate psychology as the primary determinant of male chauvinism. Socialists see the social formation as shaping individual behaviour and psyche. Whichever analysis is offered, the term, as it is descriptive and not analytical, has the same implications: it means a man who takes up a position, either consciously or instinctively, of domination (and egotism), over and against women, by virtue merely of his status as a man.

(3) Sexism and 'Patriarchy'

'Sexism', as a term, has gained increasing currency, as 'male chauvinism' (as a term) has somewhat declined. The concept is a clear analogy with 'racism' and indicates the inferiorization (attitudinal and actual) of one sex by the other. A society divided, divisively, along sex lines. Where male chauvinism is mostly used of individuals, sexism describes a whole society and social culture. One of the fullest explorations of the concept is Kate Millet's 'theory of sexual politics' or her 'notes towards a theory of patriarchy' in her recent book *Sexual Politics*.[8] 'Patriarchy' is used – slightly loosely – to mean not the rule of the father but, more generally, the rule of men. Kate Millet establishes that 'patriarchy' is a 'universal (geographical and historical) mode of power relationships' and domination.

7. New York Radical Feminist Manifesto, Cellestine Ware: op. cit., pp. 58–9.
8. Kate Millet: *Sexual Politics*, Doubleday Inc. 1970. See pp.82–4. for a slightly fuller discussion of her thesis.

She establishes that within 'patriarchy' the omnipresent system of male domination and female subjugation is achieved through socializing, perpetrated through ideological means, and maintained by institutional methods. Men are dominant by habit (the effect of psychology, socialization and ideology) and when necessary by force (they control the economy, the state and its agents, e.g. the army, and they have a monopoly on sexual violence). According to this thesis 'patriarchy' is all-pervasive: it penetrates class divisions, different societies, historical epochs. Its chief institution is the family: having the shakiest of biological foundations, 'patriarchy' must rely instead on 'inherited' culture and the training of the young. It endures as a power system because it is so well entrenched that it hardly needs to be visible, invoking the 'natural' it claims to be irrevocable. Different societies have never offered real alternatives: 'Perhaps patriarchy's greatest psychological weapon is simply its universality and longevity. A referent scarcely exists with which it might be contrasted or by which it might be confuted.'[9] Patriarchy endures because it endures.

'Patriarchy' then is the sexual politics whereby men establish their power and maintain control. All societies and all social groups within these are 'sexist' – not in the sense that one could maintain 'all societies are racist', but in the far more fundamental sense that their entire organization, at every level, is predicated on the domination of one sex by the other. Specific variations are less significant than the general truth.

(4) Feminism

Feminism has been variously defined and is currently loosely used to indicate anyone who strongly supports the rights of women – to emancipation, liberation or equality. A stricter definition is the one negatively postulated by Simone de Beauvoir in her autobiography *Force of Circumstances*.

I never cherished any illusion of changing woman's condition; it depends on the future of labour in the world; it will change

9. Kate Millet: op. cit., p. 58.

significantly only at the price of a revolution in production. That is why I avoided falling into the trap of 'feminism'.[10]

Today, it is, I believe, only 'liberal feminists' who 'cherish the illusion' that social equality can be achieved in a democratic capitalist country without a revolution; 'radical feminists' believe that it can be achieved nowhere without the feminist revolution being paramount. But liberal feminism and radical feminism do share the position that women's oppression can be fought independently of other oppressions, whereas Women's Liberationists who follow a materialist analysis, as does Simone de Beauvoir, believe it is a central, and yet intrinsic part of a larger revolutionary struggle for changing the dominant mode of production from capitalism to socialism and finally communism. Radical feminists are now inclined to re-establish this distinction as they establish their theory, so that we can say 'feminism' is the belief that women's oppression is first, foremost, and separable from any particular historical context.

10. Simone de Beauvoir: *Force of Circumstances,* André Deutsch, 1965, p. 192.

Chapter Three

The Politics of Women's Liberation: 1

The Past and the Present ...

As we saw in Chapter One, there are crucial links between the Youth Movements and Women's Liberation: both groups are embattled on the ideological plane where, as the middle-class agents and objects of the consumer 'sell' and future fabricators of the necessary consensus, they are in a position to be most aware of its meaning. But after this initial similarity women find themselves on very different terrain. Their struggle cannot remain (or even be preoccupied) with ideological issues alone but must extend to an attack on all the ramifications of oppression. Economically, women are the most highly exploited group; they are also the most psychically determined as inferior. This is, of course, their position *within* each race or class. But as a sex, despite national, racial or class differences, they share an overall inferiorization which is total.

The main thing to stress at this juncture is the complexity of the political attitudes and actions that have to match such an inclusive problem. When one has to contend with oppression in every sector, there is room, initially, for all forms of political groups or attitudes to move in. Although it is developing its own politics of liberation and feminism, Women's Liberation includes within its somewhat shadowy circumference most political positions developed during the sixties and before.

Anarchism

The 'politics of experience' initiated its own particular cults and saw to a recrudescence of previous political forms. Anarchism, for instance, had a further hey-day in the sixties.

Anarchism, in its fight for the freedom of every individual from any form of organization (hierarchic or 'democratic') has always given a generous place to women in its undifferentiating movement. Its overriding belief in the individual allows this. Every anarchist validates his or her revolutionary politics in his or her private actions and in every aspect of his or her personal life. People think of anarchism as chaos. This is too crude; but within this stress on private liberation and individual freedom there is a necessary randomness which aims a blow at anything in its way. No political system is better than any other for all are 'systems' and therein lies the error. This belief clearly has a strong appeal to women: privatized in their isolated family lives, individual freedom seems the natural horizon for which to strive. Liberation, in anarchist terms, expresses itself as a release of all one's dammed-up psychic energies: probably no one feels the need for this more than a woman. Anarchism's inclusive and random aspect qualifies everyone and legitimizes everything that is counter-system: there is no need to try to work out the whole oppression of women, no need to organize.... Individuals and a number of small groups within Women's Liberation are testing the possibility of these politics. Certainly it frees them personally from the cultural constraints of bourgeois society: they are brave and violent, without a care for the opinions of others – the obverse, in other words, of the nice 'true' woman.[1]

1. See, for instance, Germaine Greer: *The Female Eunuch*, 1970. This book is written from the anarchist individualist stance, the Hippie 'my life is the truth of your life'. It elects to be alone when people are coming together in a social and political movement, so that despite the book's many pertinent insights it dates itself as it appears – despite its stunning success it is neither 'before' nor 'behind' its time, simply *outside* it (or in the colloquial sense 'of' the moment).

Terrorism

The activities of the anarchist groups coincide in some respects with those of tightly organized 'terrorists'. These groups are a band of closely-knit militants aiming at symbolic violent action (in other contexts, kidnappings and isolated bombings). Certain feminist groups are based on comparable concepts – striking a blow when and how one can at the institutions and expressions of male chauvinism.

Spontaneism

A line runs from the subjectivism of the 'politics of experience' through the subjective 'terrorism' of the anarchists to the objective terrorism of the 'terrorists'. This line is a belief in spontaneity, whether the spontaneity of 'feelings' or the spontaneity of violence. Spontaneity is a mode which women are particularly liable to develop. On the one hand, bourgeois society has always allowed them, as the guardians of the 'natural' and of the 'proper' emotions (or what have you), *precisely to be spontaneous* – it is an assertion of beautiful femininity to burst (with seeming or seemly irrelevance) into tears, to show one's feelings by never being calculating, to intuit where men comprehend. . . . On the other hand, spontaneity (as a political concept) allows precisely the overthrow of all this *in the same terms*. In extremities of random violence or in the breaking of cultural taboos, feminists turn femininity on its head. The danger is that tossing a coin a second time one may land up with the same side one started with.

Spontaneist-terrorists model *themselves* as rocks to throw at the walls of bourgeois society. Their actions are good in so far as they never allow women to underestimate themselves and their potential: but they are bad in so far as they definitely underestimate the strength of the walls.

Furthermore, it is precisely in spontaneism that the movement reveals the dangers still inherent in its own class-nature.

It is nearly always middle-class intellectuals who become in-
fatuated with the type of personal, individual liberation which
takes this form, who find the seductive opposite to their own
repressed or sublimated lives in the outbursts of violence or
'offensiveness'. We can see this in that it is so often the 'out-
landish' features of Women's Liberation itself that capture and
titillate the intelligentsia of the left.

This infatuation with passion can be seen to take several
forms at the moment. In New York, where some Women's
Liberation groups are collecting money to pay the fines of
the women incarcerated in the House of Detention, a liberationist friend said to me, with irony, 'This is to be the year of
the prisoner.' Many feminists claim that as society oppresses
women, all women 'criminals' are political prisoners. It is not
belittling the plight of prisoners if one points out that they
certainly don't see themselves as such. After all, politics is, in
part, a question of political consciousness. The reasons why
women are in prison, and their conditions there, are clearly
matters for Women's Liberation to concern itself with; the
maximalist analysis of their so-called political status does not
follow from this. The intellectual passion for the *enragé*
(criminal or terrorist) is also to be found in its attraction to the
'outrageous'. Sexual exploration and the assertion of sexual
freedom, particularly in the realms where it is prohibited, are
clearly crucial to any expression of liberation from the sexual
dimension of the overall oppression. Homosexuals are clearly
discriminated against socio-morally and still, to a great extent,
legally. Gay Liberation is an extremely important movement. It
is crucial that, as women, and an oppressed group, we comprehend how capitalism oppresses many varied groups: our
solidarity with Gay Liberation – gay sisters and brothers – is of
paramount importance, as is their solidarity with us. But there
is a distinction to be made between, on the one hand, solidarity and the release of the bisexual or homosexual possibilities within all of us, and, on the other, a coy flirtation
with its picturesque 'outrageousness'. There is nothing
particularly joyful about being an oppressed group, or one
that is discriminated against. Genet's plays and novels make

clear the nightmare qualities of homosexual life in a society which forbids it. Being 'turned on' by prisoners or gay people glamorizes the painful predicament and loses sight of the function of a Liberation Movement.

Sectarianism

But if these are illustrations of some of the pitfalls of spontaneism, instances of the traps set up by rigidity are no harder to find. Women's Liberation, like all the new movements of the left, is subject to the mind-forged manacles of sectarianism. Recently, in Chicago, at an open Women's Liberation meeting, a young man asked me how we, in Britain, reacted to the support shown for us by 'certain left-wing organizations who have always had a good line on the position of women'. These Trotskyists have 'always' been there, because they have never been there. There is a sort of expansive tolerance in their position, a timelessness which makes room for everything – except another sect, or an actual revolution. Their stress on 'going to the working class' (and their recent awareness that there are some women there) leads them into typical economist pursuits. As far as the women's caucuses (or independent Trotskyist Women's Liberation groups) go, at least in England, they stress above all the importance of the struggle for equal pay. There is no doubt of the significance of this issue; indeed, it may be the most crucial 'right' to press for at the moment. However, its tactical dominance over other issues should not develop into its theoretical splendid isolation.

If the Trotskyists are open-armed, the Maoists (in England at least) are tight-fisted. Their tactic seems to be to shift their entire movement wholesale into whatever political struggle holds the vanguard position at any given moment, and from there maintain their grasp by clasping their fists over the tabernacle of 'the true position'. Their definition of themselves, is their condemnation of any other group. The other day, at a public meeting of the Women's Liberation Front, Mr Manchandra (nicknamed 'the Chairman Mao of England'

and sweetly referred to by comrades as 'Man' for short) got up and announced himself as a leading member of the Women's Liberation Front. Today, *all* that group of Maoists are Women's Liberationists, as yesterday they were 'Revolutionary Students'. The gray timelessness of Trotskyism is only to be matched by the eternal chameleonism of Western Maoism.

In their Women's Liberation policies there is nothing in either group to justify ridicule. They bring with them previously developed political energies; and their newly prominent personnel – the women – are bringing fresh insights to a fresh problem – women's oppression. It is just that as sects, definitionally, they always have their theory prepared and thus there is a tendency within each to seem to be waiting for any revolutionary orphan to try on their proferred garments.

Reformism

'Reformism' is a difficult concept when it comes to Women's Liberation. There is no revolutionary theory or strategy that accords a distinct place to women's oppression and liberation. It has traditionally been held on the left that women can get 'equal rights', in a bourgeois revolution, under capitalism, and, as nobody can hope for a transcendence of this concept of equality till the achievement of socialism, political demands that women make can be accommodated in the prevailing system, and hence are 'reformist'. In other words, the idea that women 'must wait till after the revolution' has, if anything, a yet more pernicious side; what you are asking for now are just reforms and you can get these fairly easily. This position is a mirror reflection of how women's issues are seen within the bourgeois society itself, i.e. as not the real issue. Nixon can welcome the idea of a vast increase in nursery schools, abortion laws are liberalized without strain.... But for the left to accept tokenism as evidence of the weakness of the demands and not of the strength of the system is a serious error. Women's demands have always been presented as reforms; whether or not they are so (or whether or not some are so) cannot be judged in the abstract, nor even in the context of the past, but only in their new context of feminist politics. The left position that maintains unquestioningly that they are so, not only apes the attitude of bourgeois society, but also seriously underestimates the role of reformism in revolutionary politics:

Revolutionary Social-Democracy has always included the struggle for reforms as part of its activities. But it utilizes 'economic' agitation for the purpose of presenting to the government, not only demands for all sorts of measures, but also (and primarily) the demand that it cease to be an autocratic government. Moreover, it considers it its duty to present this demand to the government on the basis, not of the economic struggle *alone* but of all manifestations in general of public and political life. In a word, it subordinates the struggle for reforms, as a part of the whole, to the revolutionary struggle for freedom and socialism.[2]

Only when a revolutionary theory and strategy of women's oppression is developed that challenges our 'democratic' governments can we decide which issues are reforms and subordinate them to the struggle for freedom and socialism. In the absence of such a strategy, these 'reforms' may well turn out to be its first stepping-stones.

There are, of course, in all countries a number of groups who maintain that the granting of these reforms, the giving of equal rights, would liberate women without there being necessarily any change in the socio-economic structure. Most of these groups pre-existed radical Women's Liberation proper and, indeed, were one of its sources. Important aspects of Women's Liberation developed out of, and in growing opposition to, 'equal rights' campaigns, much as Black Power grew out of and away from the Civil Rights movements. Reformist groups of this sort, even if they direct their attention mainly to the problems of middle-class women in jobs, or to the legal dimensions of discrimination, have a place. All women are oppressed and raising the consciousness of all to

2. V. I. Lenin: *What Is To Be Done?*, Moscow, 1964, pp. 59–60.

this awareness is an important task. In this sense alone, at this stage, class differences are not what is important – it is for women to see how they are subjected as a whole that is crucial. Reformist groups document and protest against this subjection.

Chapter Four

The Politics of Women's Liberation: 2

The Present and the Future ...

In the last chapter I described the influence of some of the earlier prominent political theories on Women's Liberation and their re-deployment within it. But the need clearly is for a specific theory of women's oppression. There are currently two tendencies within the movement directed towards this aim: Radical Feminists who are developing a new theory of sexist society; and those socialists who recognize the inadequacy of past socialist theory of women's position, but who believe in the viability of its methodology for providing this analysis and for whom the class theory of society and the demand for revolution (based on this theory but giving unprecedented prominence to women's oppression) is paramount.

The size of the 'absence' of women in socialist theory and practice is immense. Where analysis has been offered clearly it has been inadequate, for the resulting practice has seriously failed to match it. In 1966, writing for a Marxist magazine, I tried to describe some of the failings within the most obvious classical texts of socialist literature. I am re-presenting this account here, as I feel it still holds good, and illustrates that though we cannot, in Women's Liberation, in any sense rely on previously developed analyses – we may be able to use them, to modify and extend.[1]

1. This section and pages 100–122 and 144–51 are a re-utilization of my article 'Women: The Longest Revolution', *New Left Review*, no. 40, December, 1966. I have made a number of minor cuts and verbal alterations.

Women in Socialist Theory

The problem of the subordination of women and the need for their liberation was recognized by all the great socialist thinkers in the nineteenth century. It is part of the classical heritage of the revolutionary movement. Yet, for most of the mid-twentieth century, the problem became a subsidiary, if not an invisible element in the preoccupations of socialists. Perhaps no other major issue was so forgotten. In England, the cultural heritage of Puritanism, always strong on the left, contributed to a widespread diffusion of essentially conservative beliefs among many who would otherwise count themselves as 'progressive'. A *locus classicus* of these attitudes was Peter Townsend's remarkable statement:

Traditionally Socialists have ignored the family or they have openly tried to weaken it – alleging nepotism and the restrictions placed upon individual fulfilment by family ties. Extreme attempts to create societies on a basis other than the family have failed dismally. It is significant that a Socialist usually addresses a colleague as 'brother' and a Communist uses the term 'comrade'. The chief means of fulfilment in life is to be a member of, and reproduce, a family. There is nothing to be gained by concealing this truth.[2]

So that when the Women's Liberation Movement first arose, it broke upon socialist consciousnesses entirely innocent (ignorant) of its necessity. How did this ignorant counter-revolution come about? How had the problem of woman's condition become an area of silence within contemporary socialism? August Bebel, whose book *Woman in the Past, Present and Future* was one of the standard texts of the German Social-Democratic Party in the early years of this century, wrote:

Every Socialist recognizes the dependance of the workman on the capitalist, and cannot understand that others, and especially the capitalists themselves, should fail to recognize it also; but the same

2. Peter Townsend: 'A society for people', in *Conviction,* ed. Norman Mackenzie, 1958, pp. 119–20.

Socialist often does not recognize the dependence of women on men because the question touches his own dear self more or less nearly.[3]

But this genre of explanation – psychologistic and moralistic – though true, is clearly inadequate. Much deeper and more structural causes have been at work. To consider these would require a major historical study which I have not attempted. But it can be said with certainty that part of the explanation for the decline in socialist debate on the subject (a decline which may, in part, have provoked the rise of Women's Liberation) lies not only in the real historical processes, but in the original weakness in the traditional discussion of the subject in the socialist classics. For while the great studies of the last century all stressed the importance of the problem, they did not *solve* it theoretically. The limitations of their approach have never subsequently been transcended.

Fourier was the most ardent and voluminous advocate of women's liberation and of sexual freedom among the early socialists. He wrote:

The change in a historical epoch can always be determined by the progress of women towards freedom, because in the relation of woman to man, of the weak to the strong, the victory of human nature over brutality is most evident. The degree of emancipation of women is the natural measure of general emancipation.[4]

Marx quoted this formulation with approval in *The Holy Family*. But, characteristic of his early writings, Marx gave it a more universal and philosophical meaning. The emancipation of women would not only be as Fourier, with his greater preoccupation with sexual liberation saw it, an index of humanization in the civic sense of the victory of humaneness over brutality, but in the more fundamental sense of the progress of the human over the animal, the cultural over the natural:

3. August Bebel: *Die Frau und der Sozialismus*, 1883, trans. H. B. Adams Walther: *Woman in the Past, Present and Future*, 1885, p. 113.
4. Charles Fourier: *Théorie des Quatre Mouvements* in *Oeuvres Complètes*, (1841), I, p. 195; cit. Karl Marx: *The Holy Family*, 1845, trans. 1956, p. 259.

The relation of man to woman is the *most natural* relation of human being to human being. It indicates, therefore, how far man's *natural* behaviour has become human, and how far his *human* essence has become a *natural* essence for him, how far his *human nature* has become *nature* for him.[5]

This theme is typical of the early Marx.

Fourier's ideas remained at the level of utopian moral injunction. Marx used and transformed them, integrating them into a philosophical critique of human history. But he retained the abstraction of Fourier's conception of the position of women as an index of general social advance. This in effect makes it merely a symbol – it accords the problem a universal importance at the cost of depriving it of its specific substance. Symbols are allusions to or derivations from something else. In Marx's early writings 'woman' becomes an anthropological entity, an ontological category, of a highly abstract kind. Contrarily, in his later work, where he is concerned with describing the family, Marx differentiates it as a phenomenon according to time and place:

It is, of course, just as absurd to hold the Teutonic-Christian form of the family to be absolute and final as it would be to apply that character to the ancient Roman, the ancient Greek, or the Eastern forms which, moreover, taken together form a series in historic development.[6]

What is striking in his later comments on the family is that the problem of women becomes submerged in the analysis of the family – women, as such, are not even mentioned! Marx thus moves from generalized philosophical formulations about women in the early writings to specific historical comments on the family in the later texts. There is a serious disjunction between the two. The common framework of both was his analysis of the economy, and of the evolution of property.

5. Karl Marx: *Private Property and Communism*, 1844, in *Early Writings*, trans. T. B. Bottomore, 1963, p. 154.
6. Karl Marx: *Capital*, I, 1867, 1961 edn, p. 490.

Engels

It was left to Engels to systematize these theses in *The Origin of the Family, Private Property and the State*, after Marx's death. Engels declared that the inequality of the sexes was probably the first antagonism within the human species. The first class antagonism 'coincides with the development of the antagonism between man and woman in the monogamous marriage, and the first class oppression with that of the female sex by the male'.[7] Basing much of his theory on Morgan's fascinating, but inaccurate, anthropological investigations, Engels had many valuable insights. Inheritance, which is the key to his economist account, was first matrilineal, but with the increase of wealth became patrilineal. This was woman's greatest single setback. The wife's fidelity becomes essential and monogamy is irrevocably established. The wife in the communistic, patriarchal family is a public servant, with monogamy she becomes a private one. Engels effectively reduces the problem of woman to her capacity to work. He therefore gave her physiological weakness as a primary cause of her oppression. He locates the moment of her exploitation at the point of transition from communal to private property. If inability to work is the cause of her inferior status, ability to work will bring her liberation:

... the emancipation of women and their equality with men are impossible and must remain so as long as women are excluded from socially productive work and restricted to housework, which is private. The emancipation of women becomes possible only when women are enabled to take part in production on a large, social, scale, and when domestic duties require their attention only to a minor degree.[8]

Or:

7. Friedrich Engels: 'The Origin of the Family, Private Property and the State', 1884, in Marx-Engels: *Selected Works*, II, 1962 edn, p. 225.
  8. ibid., II, p. 311.

The first premise for the emancipation of women is the reintroduction of the entire female sex into public industry ... this ... demands that the quality possessed by the individual family of being the economic unit of society be abolished.[9]

Engels thus finds a solution schematically appropriate to his analysis of the origin of feminine oppression. The position of women, then, in the work of Marx and Engels remains dissociated from, or subsidiary to, a discussion of the family, which is in its turn subordinated as merely a precondition of private property. Their solutions retain this overly economist stress, or enter the realm of dislocated speculation.

Bebel, Engels' disciple, attempted to provide a programmatic account of woman's oppression as such, not simply as a by-product of the evolution of the family and of private property: 'From the beginning of time oppression was the common lot of woman and the labourer... *Woman was the first human being that tasted bondage, woman was a slave before the slave existed.*'[10] He acknowledged, with Marx and Engels, the importance of physical inferiority in accounting for woman's subordination, but while stressing inheritance, added that another biological element – her maternal function – was one of the fundamental conditions that made her economically dependent on the man. This is crucial, but Bebel, too, was unable to do more than state that sexual equality was impossible without socialism. His vision of the future was a vague reverie, quite disconnected from his description of the past. The absence of a strategic concern forced him into voluntarist optimism divorced from reality. Lenin himself, although he made a number of specific suggestions, inherited a tradition of thought which simply pointed to the *a priori* equation of socialism with feminine liberation without showing concretely how it would transform woman's condition: 'Unless women are brought to take an independent part not only in political life generally, but also in daily and universal public service, it is no use talking about full and stable demo-

9. ibid., II, p. 233.
10. August Bebel: op. cit., p. 7.

cracy, let alone socialism.'[11] To this point, the liberation of women remains a normative ideal, an adjunct to socialist theory, not structurally integrated into it.

The Second Sex

The contrary is true of De Beauvoir's massive work *The Second Sex* – to this day the greatest single contribution on the subject. Here the focus is the status of women through the ages. But interestingly socialism as such emerges as a curiously contingent solution at the end of the work, in a muffled epilogue. De Beauvoir's main theoretical innovation was to fuse the 'economic' and 'reproductive' explanations of women's subordination by a psychological interpretation of both. Man asserts himself as subject and free being by opposing other consciousnesses. He is distinct from animals precisely in that he creates and invents (not in that he reproduces himself), but he tries to escape the burden of his freedom by giving himself a spurious 'immortality' in his children. He dominates woman both to imprison another consciousness which reflects his own and to provide him with children that are securely his (his fear of illegitimacy). The notions obviously have a considerable force. But they are very atemporal: it is not easy to see why socialism should modify the basic 'ontological' desire for a thing like freedom which De Beauvoir sees as the motor behind the fixation with inheritance in the property system, or the enslavement of women which derived from it. In fact she has since criticized this aspect of her book for idealism:

I should take a more materialist position today in the first volume. I should base the notion of woman as *other* and the Manichean argument it entails not on an idealistic and *a priori* struggle of consciences, but on the facts of supply and demand. This modification

11. V. I. Lenin: *The Tasks of the Proletariat in Our Revolution*, 1917, in *Collected Works*, XXIV, p. 70.

would not necessitate any changes in the subsequent development of my argument.[12]

Concurrent, however, with the idealist psychological explanation, De Beauvoir uses an orthodox economist approach. This leads to a definite evolutionism in her treatment in Volume I, which becomes a retrospective narrative of the different forms of the feminine condition in different societies through time – mainly in terms of the property system and its effects on women. To this she adds various supra-historical themes – myths of the eternal feminine, types of women through the ages, literary treatments of women – which do not modify the fundamental structure of her argument. The prospect for women's liberation at the end is quite divorced from any historical development.

Thus, the classical socialist literature on the problem of woman's condition is predominantly economist in emphasis, stressing her simple subordination to the institutions of private property. Her biological status underpins both her weakness as a producer in work relations and her importance as a possession in reproductive relations. De Beauvoir's interpretation gives both factors a psychological cast, yet the framework of discussion is an evolutionist one which nevertheless fails noticeably to project a convincing image of the future, beyond asserting that socialism will involve the liberation of women as one of its constituent 'moments'.

Kate Millet's recent book *Sexual Politics* is also written within a socialist perspective. Millet states that the most important section of her book is the initial one where she develops a theory of *patriarchy*: the sexual politics whereby men establish their power and maintain control. The rest of the book discusses the history of sexual relations from 1830–1960, the psychological contributions to a concept of the feminine, the perspectives of contemporary 'social sciences', two paradigm instances of state manipulation of the family (Nazi Germany and the USSR) and, proportionally the largest section of all, notions of women and sex revealed in

12. Simone de Beauvoir: *Force of Circumstance,* op. cit. p. 192.

nineteenth- and twentieth-century literature. Presented like
that it sounds random, but a unifying link sometimes explicitly emerges which makes it clear that these are not merely
various illustrations of a 'theory of patriarchy', but essential
contributions to its development.

Millet establishes that within patriarchy the omnipresent
system of male domination and female subjugation is achieved
through socializing, perpetuated through ideological means,
and maintained by institutional methods. Millet gives us the
symptoms of patriarchy and some of the means by which it
achieves its success; she demonstrates that might is not right,
but then, nor is it, I would contend, in itself, politics. The
ways in which patriarchy works are different from *how* it
works in the sense of the articulation of those ways. Again,
the way male domination permeates our lives obscures from
us the *different* methods by which it operates. In isolating some
of these Millet has done an invaluable job, but we still – all of
us – need to work to re-cohere these insights into a 'theory'.
From the apparently undifferentiated mass (or mess) of our
experience we have to separate the mechanisms that make it
function as such, but then we have to decipher the complex
interconnections of the complex mechanisms (or contradictions) that make up the complex whole. For me, one of the
weaknesses of Millet's study is that, although it *isolates* different mechanisms, it doesn't confront their relationships; so
we are left with a sense of the random and chaotic and *equal*
contribution of each and all to the maintenance of patriarchy;
one could add to the list or shuffle it around. It is unstruc-
tured. This does not seem to me to be accidental but inherent
in the notion of patriarchy as a political system in itself. For
one thing there can be no such thing as a *general* system. Patriarchy may seem universal, but in the first place this universality is part of the ideology by which it maintains itself, and in
the second where it does indeed have common factors through
different political systems these common factors find themselves in different combinations in all specific instances. Any
political system is always a specific aggregate. This should
make us suspicious of accepting the ideological formulations

(in this case 'universality') that the system offers us as the basis of our scientific investigation of it. Another problem; a political system is dependent upon (a part of) a specific mode of production: patriarchy, though a perpetual feature of it, is not in *itself* a mode of production, though an essential aspect of every economy, it does not dominantly determine it. In seeing patriarchy as equivalent to a class system, Millet is moving away from a socialist analysis and coming closer to a feminist one. As the book was written after the advent of the Women's Liberation Movement, this conflation is, in itself, interesting.

For it is against the inadequacy of classical socialist theory that both radical feminists and socialist women in the movement have alike reacted. It is against the background of the far cruder practices of contemporary socialist groups that the Women's Liberation Movement has been founded.

Socialist Practice and Women's Liberation

In America, the experience of the preceding and even contemporary male left (black and white) was horrific. This was also true – as pointed out earlier – of the Paris Group, slightly less true of England and Holland and, though of dubious benefit, considerably less true of Scandanavian countries. Where socialist groups have apparently 'respected' the position of women, the 'respect' has had all the implications of paternalism and mystification with which its meaning in capitalist society is redolent. Again, as in contemporary society, where 'respect' is absent, thuggishness takes its place: the wife and the prostitute.

Ellen Willis describes the initial break-away confrontation between white women and white men of the New Left in Washington back in 1969. Women's Liberation was already in existence – but in an uneasy (or unholy?) alliance with other revolutionary groups. This confrontation provoked the establishment of radical feminism, a branch of the movement having no truck with the 'compromise' and sexist politics of other radical organizations. The occasion for the confrontation was the anti-inaugural demonstrations against President Nixon. There was a woman's contingent concentrating on burning their voter's registration cards to illustrate the inefficacy of the vote to change any aspects of women's oppression in America.

Ellen Willis's impressions:

Mobe's ad. in the *Guardian* calls for an end to the war and freedom for Black and Spanish people: no mention of Women's Liberation. Women in another group want to ask men to destroy their voter cards. Apparently they have interpreted the action as a simple protest against electoral politics, rather than a specifically feminist rejection of appeasement-by-ballot.

I get the funny feeling that we're being absorbed. Will we get the chance to deliver our message, or are we just there to show our support for the important (i.e. male-oriented) branches of the Left? Our group decides to confront this issue with a speech attacking male chauvinism in the movement.

Dave Dellinger introduces the rally with a stirring denunciation of the war and racism.

'What about women, you schmuck,' I shout.

'And, uh, a special message from Women's Liberation,' he adds. Our moment comes. M., from the Washington group, stands up to speak. This isn't the protest against movement men, which is the second on the agenda, just fairly innocuous radical rhetoric – except that it's a good looking woman talking about women. The men go crazy. 'Take it off!' 'Take her off the stage and fuck her!' They yell and boo and guffaw at unwitting *double-entendres* like 'We must take to the streets.' When S. (Shulamith Firestone), who is representing the New York group, comes to the mike and announces that women will no longer participate in so-called revolution that does not include the abolition of male privilege, it sounds like a spontaneous outburst of rage (rather than like a deliberate statement of the politics of Women's Liberation). By the time we get to the voter card business, I am shaking. If radical men can be so easily provoked into acting like rednecks (a Women's Liberation group at the University of North Carolina was urinated on by male hecklers at a demonstration) what can we expect from others? What have we gotten ourselves into? Meanwhile Dellinger has been pleading with us to get off the stage, 'for your own good'. Why isn't he telling them to shut up?[13]

And from Paris, at Vincennes, the enclave of the May revolutionaries:

As we walked around we handed out leaflets, particularly to women. A crowd of about a hundred people followed us around; most of them were hostile. We had been prepared for significant opposition from men, even afraid of it; but even so were not prepared for such depth and breadth of outrage. Here were 'movement' men shouting insults at us: 'Lesbians', 'Strip', 'What you need is a good fuck . . .'[14]

Not one single left-wing movement: working-class, Black or student can offer anything to contradict this experience.[15] Radical feminism – the belief in the *primary* and paramount oppression of women was born as a phoenix from the ashes of this type of socialism. If socialism is to regain its status as *the* revolutionary politics (in addition to the scientific analysis it offers of capitalist society) it has to make good its practical sins of commission against women and its huge sin of omission – the absence of an adequate place for them in its theory. Many Women's Liberation groups have remained committed to Marxist socialism, planning to supplement a theory whose expertise in the analysis of capitalism has already developed to include the conditions for revolution in imperialized, feudal countries and, therefore, hopefully can offer insight into all forms of oppression, including that of women, an oppression which so far endures all changes in the mode of production. Radical feminist and socialist Women's Liberation groups, despite their crucially different analyses, share a revolutionary politics and this involves many of the same basic concepts.

13. *US,* New York, October 1969, pp. 99, 113–15. Also quoted by Celestine Ware: op. cit., pp. 35–7.

14. Printed in *Black Dwarf,* vol. XIV, no. 37, 5 September 1970, p. 15.

15. The experience of women in socialist countries is rarely found to be encouraging. See Millet: op. cit., for the USSR, and Chris Camarano: *Leviathan,* vol. II, no. 1, for Cuba, as two instances of Women's Liberation criticism.

Feminism

Feminism unites women at the level of their total oppression – it is all-inclusive (cf. Black Power and 'totalism'). Its politics match this: it is a total attack. The theory backs this: the first division of labour was the first formation of oppressor and oppressed – the first division of labour was between man and woman. The first domination must be given priority – it must be the first to go. This is poetic justice: what are its political implications?

Shulamith Firestone's invigorating book, *The Dialectic of Sex* is the fullest development of the theory to date. Radical feminism finds that the inadequacies within Marxist analyses of a comprehension of women's oppression, are due *not* to its chronic underdevelopment in this sphere (as Marxist women believe) but to the limitations of the theory itself. The failure is not failure of attention, but limitation of scope.

... we must enlarge historical materialism to *include* the strictly Marxian, in the same way that the physics of relativity did not invalidate Newtonian physics so much as it drew a circle around it, limiting its application – but only through comparison – to a smaller sphere. For an economic diagnosis traced to ownership of the means of production, even of the means of *re*production, does not explain everything. There is a level of reality that does not stem directly from economics. ... We can attempt to develop a materialist view of history based on sex itself.[16]

Amoeba-like, radical feminism, would ingest Marxism. The historical basis is not the economic determinism of the classes but the natural division of the sexes which precedes this. As a materialist Firestone gives full weight to the objective physiological sexual differences. Her argument proceeds thus: there is no doubt that the male and female of the species are distinct; the distinction that counts is the ability to bear children. This is not just because it has been socially exploited to oppress women, but because *in itself* it is a brutal, painful experience. Hence the revolution is not just against a specific historical

16. Shulamith Firestone: op. cit., p. 6.

form of society (e.g. capitalism), but against Nature (and its untranscended manifestations in all human culture):

> Feminists have to question, not just all of *Western* culture, but the organization of culture itself, and further, even the very organization of nature.... For feminist revolution we shall need an analysis of the dynamics of sex war as comprehensive as the Marx–Engels analysis of class antagonism was for the economic revolution. More comprehensive. For we are dealing with a larger problem, with an oppression that goes back beyond recorded history to the animal kingdom itself.[17]

As the elimination of economic classes requires the revolt of the economic 'underclass' (the proletariat), so the overthrow of the sexual classes similarly demands the revolt of its underclass (women). In both cases the revolution is not to conquer privilege but to eliminate distinction. This is the expansion of a materialist analysis, and an extension of the implications of revolution:

> We have attempted to take the class analysis one step further to its roots in the biological division of the sexes. We have not thrown out the insights of the socialists; on the contrary, radical feminism enlarges their analysis, granting it an even deeper basis in objective conditions and thereby explaining many of its insolubles.[18]

The material basis for sexual division being the reproductive system, the revolutionary means to its annihilation will be man's scientific ability to transcend it. Science conquers Nature. The ecological revolution will finally put an end to the biological base. Feminism and the new ecological technology arise together, both caused by the contradictions of the primitive and oppressed animal life that mankind lives, within the context of the possibility of vast technological improvement. Both have arisen to protest against man's refusal of what he *could* do to bring heaven closer to earth. Both, if they are frustrated, will only mean that mankind, in irretrievable conservatism, prefers hell: chronic over-population, famine, wretched hard work, pain, pregnancy, disease.... Embracing the feminist and ecological revolution would mean that

17. ibid., p. 2.
18. ibid., p. 13.

cybernation and other technological advances would end all joyless labour: the labour of the factory and of the child-bed.

A feminist revolution could be the decisive factor in establishing a new ecological balance: attention drawn to the population explosion, a shifting of emphasis from reproduction to contraception and demands for the full development of artificial reproduction would provide an alternative to the oppressions of the biological family; cybernation, by changing man's relationship to work and wages, by transforming activity from 'work' to 'play' (activity done for its own sake), would allow for a total redefinition of the economy, including the family unit in its economic capacity. The double curse, that man should till the soil by the sweat of his brow, and that woman should bear in pain and travail, would be lifted through technology to make humane living, for the first time, a possibility.[19]

Radical feminism, the revolution for the release of the oppressed majority of the world, would liberate test-tube babies, baby-farms, big-brother control, from their confinement within the horrors of 'brave new world' and 1984, and guarantee that their humane application would finally free mankind from the trap of painful biology. Thus culture would at last overcome nature and the 'ultimate revolution' would be achieved.

The analysis leads to some very pertinent insights, for instance, the shared oppression of women and children, the permeation of all cultures by a fundamental pattern of family relationships and the psychology of oppression. Firestone's castigation of many mystifications that surround woman, pregnancy, 'being in love', etc. are salutary. Yet what of the basic premise? The *Dialectic* of Sex? The extension of historical materialism? Certainly enlarging Marxist class analysis to incorporate the division of the sexes is materialist, but that doesn't make it either historical or dialectical. In fact, it precisely returns us to the type of dualistic concept that preceded the discovery of dialectical materialism. That the technological-ecological revolution of the future will transcend and harmonize the biological and cultural dualities – male/female

19. ibid., p. 228–9.

– in no sense makes that a dialectical moment. Dialectical materialism posits a complex (not dualistic) structure in which all elements are in contradiction to each other; at some point these contradictions can coalesce, explode and be overcome but the new fusion will enter into contradiction with something else. Human society is, and always will be, full of contradictions. Never can the complex structure become a simple whole in the way Firestone suggests:

> What we shall have in the next cultural revolution is the reintegration of the Male (Technological Mode) with the Female (Aesthetic Mode), to create an androgynous culture surpassing the highs of either cultural stream, or even of the sum of their integrations. More than a marriage, rather an abolition of the cultural categories themselves, a mutual cancelation – a matter-antimatter explosion, ending with a poof! culture itself. We shall not miss it. We shall no longer need it: by then humanity will have mastered nature totally, will have realized in *actuality* its dreams.[20]

The theory is no more *historical* than it is dialectical. To say that sex dualism was the first oppression and that it underlies all oppression may be true, but it is a general, non-specific truth, it is simplistic materialism, no more. After all we can say there has always been a master class and a servant class, but it does matter *how* these function (whether they are feudal landlords and peasants, capitalists and the working class or so on); there have always been classes, as there have always been sexes, how do these operate within any given, specific society? Without such knowledge (historical materialism) we have not the means of overcoming them. Nothing but this knowledge, and revolutionary action based upon it, determines the fate of technology – towards freedom or towards 1984.

Marxism has not been sufficiently developed to incorporate new scientific discoveries (e.g. those of Freud, which Firestone rightly finds so important). Finding a theory that explains the oppression of women will most likely involve us in rejecting some of the statements made by Marx and Marxists – rejecting them *because* we are utilizing the methods of Marxist

20. ibid., p. 214.

dialectical materialism. As Lenin commented we must not 'sacrifice the method of Engels to the letter of Engels'.

Engels says explicitly that with each epoch-making discovery even in the sphere of natural science ('not to speak of the history of mankind'), materialism has to change its form. (Engels: *Ludwig Feuerbach*). Hence, a revision of the 'form' of Engels' materialism, a revision of his natural-philosophical propositions is not only not 'revisionism', in the accepted meaning of the term, but, on the contrary, is demanded by Marxism.[21]

The Marxist method must indeed be made to take in the new scientific discoveries and the new social forces such as feminism, but it must be used historically and dialectically. Firestone has thrown out both these in a return to a dualistic base and its monistic solution – this is 'materialism below, idealist above'.

Where are we Going?

Perhaps in the future, the biggest single theoretical battle will have to be that between liberationists with a socialist analysis, and feminists with a 'radical feminist' analysis. But that future has come too soon. The conflict is premature because neither group has yet developed a 'theory'. The 'practice' which is that theory's condition of production has only just begun. This is not an argument for 'holding our horses' and such-like timidities; the 'immaturity' of a movement should never be an excuse for not forging ahead – it is precisely 'immature' just so long as we refuse to push on. But it *is* an argument for the simultaneous necessity of radical feminist consciousness and of the development of a socialist analysis of the oppression of women.

The main reason why the battle has been engaged prematurely, belongs to the prehistory of the Women's Liberation Movement. Responsibility largely lies with the nature of the socialist groups in the Western World during the sixties. The

21. V. I. Lenin; 'The Recent Revolution in Natural Sciences and Philosophical Idealism', *Collected Works*, vol. XIV, p. 251.

much greater flexibility they displayed in analysing new
revolutionary groups – Blacks, students and youth – often fell
between the two stools of over-rapid and crude assimilation of
them to dogmatic socialist positions, or developed outside the
reaches of socialist theory altogether. The same duality marks,
in this respect, the Women's Movement. The rejection of
socialism by radical feminists is only the other side of the same
coin as the over-hasty *rush* into revolutionary socialism by
those left-wing sisters who have always hovered around the
edges without a 'place' within it – either theoretically or
practically. The demand that 'what we've got to understand is
the relationship of Women's Liberation to socialism' is twin-
sister to 'socialism has nothing to offer us'. It is not 'our
relationship' to socialism that should ever be the question –
it is the use of scientific socialism as a method of analysing the
specific nature of our oppression and hence our revolutionary
role. Such a method, I believe, needs the understanding of
radical feminism quite as much as of the previously developed
socialist theories.

Feminist consciousness is the material with which our
politics must work, if it is to develop. The Women's Liberation Movement is at the stage of organizing our 'instinct' of
our oppression as women, into a consciousness of its meaning.
This will become a rational consciousness as we come to
understand the objective conditions which determine this
oppression. At the moment, the essential 'instinct' coexists
with the possibilities for transforming it into rational consciousness. The 'instinct' expresses itself as all our protests
against *every* manifestation of our oppression – it is here that
the jokey, spontaneous bra-burning, the smoke-bombing of
Miss World competitions, descriptions of the misery of housework and of the degradation of women's jobs have their
place, as machine-breaking and descriptions of the 'real life'
of the workers in the nineteenth century had a place in the
formation of working-class consciousness. It is as though we
suddenly, out of the blue-mists of mystification, see what is
being done to us. Socialists in the movement who want to
combat the feminist instinct forget that they will be charging

empty-handed against their own would-be weapons. We *do* have to experience the implications of our own oppression.[22]

However, where socialists would by-pass the exploration of oppression to pounce upon a theory that fits in with earlier socialist analyses (such a theory is inevitably idealist), radical feminists construct too rigid a theory from feminist instinct. The notion of undifferentiated male domination from the earliest to the latest times simply gives a theoretical form to the way oppression is usually experienced. It is also somewhat equivalent to a worker seeing the employer himself as the only enemy, simply because he seems directly responsible for the individual exploitation. This is an *aspect* of the oppression, or exploitation and should not be ignored, but nor should it be made to stand for the total situation. On the other hand, those who counter the radical feminist analysis of men as the oppressor, shirk a very important aspect of the oppression if they simply say, 'no, it's *not* men, it's the system'. The two clearly interrelate, and feminist instinct is correct in experiencing the supremacist role that men play as part of the overall oppression.

I think, then, that we have to develop our feminist consciousness to the full, and at the same time transform it by beginning a scientific socialist analysis of our oppression. The two processes must go on simultaneously – feminist consciousness will not 'naturally' develop into socialism, nor should it: the two are coextensive and must be worked on together. If we simply develop feminist consciousness (as radical feminists suggest) we will get, not political consciousness,

22. Shulamith Firestone's (op. cit., pp. 40–41) criticisms have a true-enough ring: 'Politico women are unable to evolve an authentic politics because they have never truly confronted their oppression *as women* in a gut way. Their inability to originate a feminist leftist analysis of their own, their need to tie their issue at all times to some "primary struggle" rather than seeing it as central, or even revolutionary in itself, is derived directly from their lingering feelings of inferiority as women. Their inability to put their own needs first, their need for male approval ... – to legitimate them politically, renders them incapable of breaking from other movements when necessary, and this consigns them to mere left reformism, lack of originality, and, ultimately, political sterility.'

but the equivalent of national chauvinism among Third World nations or economism among working-class organizations; simply a self-directed gaze, that sees only the internal workings of one segment; only this segment's self-interest. Political consciousness responds to all forms of oppression.

On the other hand, if our socialist 'theories' ignore our feminist consciousness they *cannot* understand the specific nature of our oppression as women. Having not *worked* on this terrain, any 'theory' here immediately falls for idealist bourgeois ideology, as this is the dominant ideology under capitalism, and there is, in this case, a refusal of the experience and analysis of oppression that would countermand it.

Radical feminists and those socialists in the movement who deny the importance of feminist consciousness *present* their positions as polar opposites, but, if isolated, both end up, at the same point, succumbing to the chief tenets of bourgeois thought: empiricism and idealism. Radical feminism makes a 'theory' of the concrete *experience* of oppression, and those we might call 'abstract socialists' evade the specific oppression of women and *idealize* the *role* of the oppressed.

This debate, as I have presented it, probably seems rather remote from most people's experience of disagreements with the movement; perhaps tabulating some of the arguments on either side will give it the necessary concreteness.

Radical Feminists	*Abstract Socialists*
Men are the oppressors.	Men are not the oppressors: it's the system.
All societies have been male supremacist.	Capitalism oppresses women.
It starts with a psychological power struggle – which men win.	It starts with private property.
Socialism has nothing to offer us.	We've got to discover 'our relationship' to socialism.

Radical Feminists	*Abstract Socialists*
Socialist countries oppress women.	The scene isn't too good in socialist countries for women – but that's because women's liberation wasn't part of the revolutionary struggle.
What we want, is all women to unite against men and male-dominated society.	It's most necessary to convince men of the importance of our struggle. They are oppressed by their roles too.
We want to liberate women from male oppression.	All people are alienated under capitalism, we want to liberate everybody to become 'whole people'.

Both positions are possibly right together, both are certainly wrong apart. Hence, the battle is premature. 'Radical feminism', in capturing the *experience* of oppression, starts to grapple with the ideological and psychological oppression of women. 'Abstract socialism' points to the economic oppression and does, in a hackneyed form, indicate the importance of the relationships between different groups, and the complexities of a specific society.

If we could start to use the methods of scientific socialism on the material of our oppression, whose most advanced expression is feminism, then, truly a 'theory' might start to evolve from our practice.

It is true that to date the socialist countries still tend to discriminate against women – it is hardly surprising given the length and nature of their prehistory. But what is more important is that the oppression of women is *intrinsic* to the capitalist system – as it is *not* to the socialist. We have to see why and how our oppression is structurally necessary today in order to fight for its overthrow. As it is structurally necessary, this struggle will involve, and be a part of, the struggle of all people who are comparably and necessarily oppressed. This is not the generality of 'all people are alienated under capitalism' (or all men and women), but applies to specific groups. The relationship between these is a crucial means of understanding ourselves – we cannot comprehend our own oppression in isolation.

Feminism, then, is the terrain on which a socialist analysis works. It is, by definition, available to all women, whatever their class or previous political position: *it is about being women.* In itself it can produce no revolutionary ideology, any more than the consciousness of workers *on its own*, can produce this:

Since there can be no talk of an independent ideology formulated by the working masses themselves in the process of their movement, the *only* choice is – either bourgeois or socialist ideology. There is no middle course (for mankind has not created a 'third' ideology, and, moreover, in a society torn by class antagonisms there can never be a non-class or an above-class ideology). Hence to belittle the socialist ideology *in any way, to turn aside from it in the slightest degree,* means to strengthen bourgeois ideology.[23]

The trouble is, that 'socialists' try to prevent feminists from having their 'feminist consciousness' by asking them to subscribe to a working-class 'ideology' – which can exist no more than feminist ideology. All oppressed groups – workers, women, colonized – can have their oppressed consciousness, but the ideology they propagate must be either that that is dominant in the society that oppresses them (bourgeois ideology), or that that they have consciously espoused for the society that will overthrow this (socialist ideology). The oppressed consciousness of all groups contributes to the nature of this socialist ideology – if any oppressed awareness is missing from its formation that is its loss. Feminist consciousness has been inadequately represented in the formation of socialist ideology, as the oppression of women has, so far, been inadequately combatted in socialist revolutions.

23. V. I. Lenin: *What is To Be Done?* op. cit., p. 39.

Part Two

THE OPPRESSION
OF WOMEN

Chapter Five

The Position of Women: 1

Radical feminism attempts to solve the problem of analysing the oppression of women by making it *the* problem. The largest, first and foremost. While such a theory remains descriptive of the experience, it *does* nevertheless stress the magnitude of the problem. What we need is a theory that is at once large enough and yet is capable of being specific. We have to see *why* women have always been oppressed, and *how* they are oppressed now, and how differently elsewhere. As radical feminists demand, we must dedicate ourselves to a theory of the oppression of all women and yet, at the same time, not lose sight of the historical specificity in the general statement. We should ask the feminist questions, but try to come up with some Marxist answers.

The situation of women is different from that of any other oppressed social group: they are half of the human species. In some ways they are exploited and oppressed like, and along with, other exploited classes or oppressed groups – the working-class, Blacks, etc.... Until there is a revolution in production, the labour situation will prescribe women's situation within the world of men. But women are offered a universe of their own: the family. Women are exploited at work, and relegated to the home: the two positions compound their oppression. Their subservience in production is obscured by their assumed dominance in their own world – the family. What is the family? And what are the actual functions that a woman fulfils within it? Like woman herself, the family appears as a natural object, but is actually a cultural creation. There is nothing inevitable about the form or role of the family, any more than there is about the character or role of women. It is the function of ideology to present these given social types as aspects of Nature itself. Both can be exalted, paradoxically, as ideals. The 'true' woman and the 'true' family are images of peace and plenty: in actuality they may both be sites of violence and despair. The apparently natural condition can be made to appear more attractive than the arduous advance of human beings towards culture. But what Marx wrote about the bourgeois myths of the Golden Ancient World describes precisely women's realm.

... in one way the child-like world of the ancients appears to be superior; and this is so, insofar as we seek for closed shape, form and established limitation. The ancients provide a narrow satis-faction, whereas the modern world leaves us unsatisfied, or, where it appears to be satisfied with itself, is *vulgar* and *mean*.[1]

The ideology of 'woman' presents her as an undifferentiated whole – 'a woman', alike the world over, eternally the same. Likewise the 'concept' of the family is of a unit that endures across time and space, there have always been families. ... Within its supposed permanent structure, eternal woman finds her place. So the notion goes. ... Any analysis of woman, and of the family, must uncoil this ideological concept of their per-manence and of their unification into an monolithic whole, mother and child, a woman's place ... her natural destiny. Theoretical analysis and revolutionary action must de-structure and destroy the inevitability of this combination.

Past socialist theory has failed to differentiate woman's condition into its separate structures, which together form a complex – not a simple – unity. To do this will mean rejecting the idea that woman's condition can be deduced derivatively from the economy (Engels), or equated symbolically with society (early Marx). Rather, it must be seen as a *specific* struc-ture, which is a unity of different elements. The variations of woman's condition throughout history will be the result of different combinations of these elements – we will thus have

1. Karl Marx: *Pre-Capitalist Economic Formations,* ed. Hobsbawm, Lawrence & Wishart, 1964, p. 85.

not a linear narrative of economic development (De Beauvoir) for the elements will be combined in different ways at different times. In a complex totality each independent sector has its own autonomous reality though each is ultimately, but only ultimately, determined by the economic factor. This complex totality means that no contradiction in society is ever simple. As each sector can move at a different pace, the synthesis of the different time-scales in the total structure means that sometimes contradictions cancel each other out, and sometimes they reinforce one another. Because the unity of woman's condition at any time is in this way the product of several structures, moving at different paces, it is always 'overdetermined'.[2]

The key structures of woman's situation can be listed as follows: Production, Reproduction, Sexuality and the Socialization of Children. The concrete combination of these produce the 'complex unity' of her position; but each separate structure may have reached a different 'moment' at any given historical time. Each then must be examined separately in order to see what the present unity is, and how it might be changed. The notes that follow do not pretend to give a historical account of each sector. They are only concerned with some general reflections on the different roles of women and some of their interconnections.

1. Production

The biological differentiation of the sexes into male and female and the division of labour that is based on this have *seemed*, throughout history, an interlocked necessity. Anatomically smaller and weaker, woman's physiology and her psychobiological metabolism appear to render her a less useful

2. See Louis Althusser: 'Contradiction and Overdetermination', in *For Marx*, Allen Lane, London, 1970. To describe the movement of this complexity, as I have mentioned above, Althusser uses the Freudian term 'overdetermination'. The phrase *'unité de rupture'* (mentioned below) refers to the moment when the contradictions so reinforce one another as to coalesce into the conditions for a revolutionary change.

member of a work-force. It is always stressed how, particularly
in the early stages of social development, man's physical
superiority gave him the means of conquest over nature which
was denied to women. Once woman was accorded the menial
tasks involved in maintenance while man undertook conquest
and creation, she became an aspect of the things preserved:
private property and children. Marx, Engels, Bebel, De
Beauvoir – the major socialist writers on the subject – link the
confirmation and continuation of woman's oppression after
the establishment of her physical inferiority for hard manual
work with the advent of private property. But woman's
physical weakness has never prevented her from performing
work as such (quite apart from bringing up children) – only
specific types of work, in specific societies. In Primitive,
Ancient, Oriental, Medieval and Capitalist societies, the
volume of work performed by women has always been considerable (it has usually been much more than this). It is only
its form that is in question. Domestic labour, even today, is
enormous if quantified in terms of productive labour.[3] It has
been calculated in Sweden, that 2,340 million hours a year are
spent by women in housework compared with 1,290 million
hours in industry. The Chase Manhattan Bank estimated a
woman's overall working week averaged 99.6 hours. In any
case women's physique alone has never permanently or even
predominantly relegated them to menial domestic chores. In
many peasant societies, women have worked in the fields as
much as, or more than, men.

3. Apologists who make out that housework, though time-consuming,
is light and relatively enjoyable, are refusing to acknowledge the dull and
degrading routine it entails. Lenin commented crisply: 'You all know that
even when women have full rights, they still remain factually down-
trodden because all housework is left to them. In most cases housework is
the most unproductive, the most barbarous and the most arduous work a
woman can do. It is exceptionally petty and does not include anything
that would in any way promote the development of the woman.' (*Collected Works*, vol. XXX, p. 43.)

Physical Weakness and Coercion

The assumption behind most socialist analyses is that the crucial factor starting the whole development of feminine subordination was women's lesser capacity for demanding physical work. But, in fact, this is a major oversimplification. Even in these terms, historically it has been woman's lesser capacity for violence as well as for work, that has determined her subordination. In most societies woman has not only been less able than man to perform arduous kinds of work, she has also been less able to fight. Man not only has the strength to assert himself against nature, but also against his fellows. *Social coercion* has interplayed with the straightforward division of labour, based on biological capacity, to a much greater extent than is generally admitted. Women have been *forced* to do 'women's work'. Of course, this force may not be actualized as direct aggression. In primitive societies women's lesser physical suitability for the hunt is assumed to be evident. In agricultural societies where women's inferiority is socially instituted, they are given the arduous task of tilling and cultivation. For this coercion is necessary. In developed civilizations, and more complex societies, woman's physical deficiencies again become relevant. Women are thought to be of no use either for war or in the construction of cities. But with early industrialization, coercion once more becomes important. As Marx wrote: 'insofar as machinery dispenses with muscular power, it becomes a means of employing labourers of slight muscular strength, and those whose bodily development is incomplete, but whose limbs are all the more supple. The labour of women and children was, therefore, the first thing sought for by capitalists who used machinery'.[4]

René Dumont points out that in many zones of tropical Africa today men are often idle, while women are forced to work all day. 'The African woman experiences a three-fold servitude: through forced marriage; through her dowry and polygamy, which increases the leisure time of men and simultaneously their social prestige; and finally through the very

4. Karl Marx: *Capital*, I, p. 394.

unequal division of labour'[5] (This exploitation has no 'natural' source whatever. Women may perform their 'heavy' duties in contemporary African peasant societies, not for fear of physical reprisal by their men, but because these duties are 'customary' and built into the role structures of the society. A further point is that coercion implies a different relationship from coercer to coerced than does exploitation. It is political rather than economic. In describing coercion Marx said that the master treated the slave or serf as the 'inorganic and natural condition of its own reproduction'. That is to say, labour itself becomes like other natural things – cattle or soil:

The original conditions of production appear as natural pre-requisites, *natural conditions of the existence of the producer*, just as his living body, however reproduced and developed by him, is not originally established by himself, but appears as his *prerequisite*.[6]

This is pre-eminently woman's condition. For far from woman's *physical* weakness removing her from productive work, her *social* weakness has in these cases evidently made her the major slave of it.

This truth, elementary though it may seem, has nevertheless been constantly ignored by socialist writers on the subject, with the result that there is an unfounded optimism in their predictions of the future. For, if it is just the biological in-capacity for the hardest physical work which has determined the subordination of women, then the prospect of an advanced machine technology, abolishing the need for strenuous physical exertion, would seem to promise, therefore, the liberation of women. For a moment industrialization itself thus seems to herald women's liberation. Engels, for instance, wrote:

The first premise for the emancipation of women is the re-introduction of the entire female sex into public industry. . . . And this has become possible only as a result of modern large-scale industry, which not only permits of the participation of women in production in large numbers, but actually calls for it and, moreover

5. René Dumont: *L'Afrique Noire est Mal Partie,* 1962, p. 210.
6. Karl Marx: *Precapitalist Economic Formations,* op. cit., p. 87.

strives to convert private domestic work also into a public industry.[7]

What Marx said of early industrialism is no less, but also *no more* true of an automated society:

... it is obvious that the fact of the collective working group being composed of individuals of both sexes and all ages, must necessarily, *under suitable conditions,* become a source of human development; although in its spontaneously developed, brutal, capitalist form, where the labourer exists for the process of production, and not the process of production for the labourer, that fact is a pestiferous source of corruption and slavery.'[8]

Industrial labour and automated technology both promise the preconditions for women's liberation alongside man's – but no more than the preconditions. It is only too obvious that the advent of industrialization has not so far freed women in this sense, either in the West or in the East. De Beauvoir hoped that automation would make a decisive, qualitative difference by abolishing altogether the physical differential between the sexes. But any reliance on this in itself accords an independent role to technique which history does not justify. Under capitalism, automation could possibly lead to an ever-growing structural unemployment which would expel women (along with immigrants) – the latest and least integrated recruits to the labour force and ideologically the most expendable for a bourgeois society – from production after only a brief interlude in it. Technology is mediated by the total structure, and it is this which will determine woman's future in work relations. It is the relationship between the social forces and technology that Firestone's 'ecological' revolution ultimately ignores.

Physical deficiency is not now, any more than in the past, a sufficient explanation of woman's relegation to inferior status. Coercion has been ameliorated to an ideology shared by both sexes. Commenting on the results of her questionnaire of working women, Viola Klein notes: 'There is no trace of

7. Friedrich Engels: op. cit., II, pp. 233, 311.
8. Karl Marx: *Capital,* I, p. 394.

feminine egalitarianism – militant or otherwise – in any of the women's answers to the questionnaire; nor is it even implicitly assumed that women have a "Right to Work".[9] Denied, or refusing, a role in *production*, woman does not even create the preconditions of her liberation. But even her presence in the work force does not erode her oppression in the family.

2. The Reproduction of Children

Women's absence from the critical sector of production historically, of course, has been caused not just by their assumed physical weakness in a context of coercion – but also by their role in reproduction. Maternity necessitates withdrawals from work, but this is not a decisive phenomenon. It is rather women's role in reproduction which has become, in capitalist society at least, the spiritual 'complement' of men's role in production. Bearing children, bringing them up, and maintaining the home – these form the core of woman's natural vocation, in this ideology. This belief has attained great force because of the seeming universality of the family as a human institution. There is little doubt that Marxist analyses have underplayed the fundamental problems posed here. The complete failure to give any operative content to the slogan of 'abolition' of the family is striking evidence of this (as well as of the vacuity of the notion).

The biological function of maternity is a universal, atemporal fact, and as such has seemed to escape the categories of Marxist historical analysis. However, from it is made to follow the so-called stability and omnipresence of the family, if in very different forms.[10] Once this is accepted, women's social subordination – however emphasized as an honourable, but different role (cf. the equal-but-'separate' ideologies of

9. Viola Klein: 'Working Wives', *Institute of Personnel Management Occasional Papers*, no. 15, 1960, p. 13.

10. Philippe Ariès in *Centuries of Childhood*, 1962, shows that though the family may in some form always have existed it was often submerged under more forceful structures. In fact according to Ariès it has only acquired its present significance with the advent of industrialization.

Southern racists) – can be seen to follow inevitably as an *insurmountable* bio-historical fact. The causal chain then goes: maternity, family, absence from production and public life, sexual inequality.

The lynch-pin in this line of argument is the idea of the family. The notion that 'family' and 'society' are virtually co-extensive or that an advanced society not founded on the nuclear family is now inconceivable, despite revolutionary posturings to the contrary, is still widespread. It can only be seriously discussed by asking just what the family is – or rather what women's role in the family is. Once this is done, the problem appears in quite a new light. For it is obvious that woman's role in the family – primitive, feudal or bourgeois – partakes of three quite different structures: reproduction, sexuality, and the socialization of children. These are historically, not intrinsically, related to each other in the present modern family. We can easily see that they needn't be. For instance, biological parentage is not necessarily identical with social parentage (adoption). Thus it is essential to discuss not the family as an unanalysed entity, but the separate *structures* which today compose it but which tomorrow may be decomposed into a new pattern.

As I have said, reproduction is seen as an apparently constant atemporal phenomenon – part of biology rather than history. In fact this is an illusion. What is true is that the 'mode of reproduction' does not vary with the 'mode of production'; it can remain effectively the same through a number of different modes of production. For it has been defined till now by its uncontrollable, natural character and to this extent has been an unmodified biological fact. As long as reproduction remained a natural phenomenon, of course, women were effectively doomed to social exploitation. In any sense, they were not 'masters' of a large part of their lives. They had no choice as to whether or how often they gave birth to children (apart from precarious methods of contraception or repeated dangerous abortions); their existence was essentially subject to biological processes outside their control.

Contraception

Contraception which was finally invented as a rational technique only in the nineteenth century was thus an innovation of
world-historic importance. It is only just now beginning to
show what immense consequences it could have, in the form
of the Pill. For what it means is that at last the mode of reproduction potentially could be transformed. Once child-
bearing becomes totally voluntary (how much so is it in the
West, even today?) its significance is fundamentally different.
It need no longer be the sole or ultimate vocation of woman;
it becomes one option among others.

History is the development of man's transformation of
nature, and thereby of himself – of human nature – in different
modes of production. Today there are the technical possibilities for the transformation and 'humanization' of the
most natural part of human culture. This is what a change in
the mode of reproduction could mean.

We are far from this state of affairs yet. In Italy the sale of
contraceptives remains illegal. In many countries it is difficult
to get reliable means. The oral contraceptive is still the
privilege of a moneyed minority in a few western countries.
Even here the progress has been realized in a typically conservative and exploitative form. It is made only for women,
who are thus 'guinea-pigs' in a venture which involves both
sexes.

The fact of overwhelming importance is that easily available
contraception threatens to dissociate sexual from reproductive
experience – which all contemporary ideology tries to make
inseparable, as the *raison d'être* of the family.

Reproduction and Production

At present, reproduction in our society is often a kind of sad
mimicry of production. Work in a capitalist society is an
alienation of labour in the making of a social product which is
confiscated by capital. But it can still sometimes be a real act of
creation, purposive and responsible, even in the conditions of

the worst exploitation. Maternity is often a caricature of this. The biological product – the child – is treated as if it were a solid product. Parenthood becomes a kind of substitute for work, an activity in which the child is seen as an object created by the mother, in the same way as a commodity is created by a worker. Naturally, the child does not literally escape, but the mother's alienation can be much worse than that of the worker whose product is appropriated by the boss. The child as an autonomous person, inevitably threatens the activity which claims to create it continually merely as a *possession* of the parent. Possessions are felt as extensions of the self. The child as a possession is supremely this. Anything the child does is therefore a threat to the mother herself, who has renounced her autonomy through this misconception of her reproductive role. There are few more precarious ventures on which to base a life.

Furthermore even if the woman has emotional control over her child, legally and economically both she and it are subject to the father. The social cult of maternity is matched by the real socio-economic powerlessness of the mother. The psychological and practical benefits men receive from this are obvious. The converse of woman's quest for creation in the child is man's retreat from his work into the family: 'When we come home, we lay aside our mask and drop our tools, and are no longer lawyers, sailors, soldiers, statesmen, clergymen, but only men. We fall again into our most human relations, which, after all, are the whole of what belongs to us as we are ourselves.'[11]

Unlike her non-productive status, her capacity for maternity *is* a definition of woman. But it is only a physiological definition. Yet so long as it is allowed to remain a substitute for action and creativity, and the home an area of relaxation for men, woman will remain confined to the species, to her universal and natural condition.

11. J. A. Froude: *Nemesis of Faith*, 1849, p. 103.

3. Sexuality

Sexuality has traditionally been the most tabooed dimension
of women's situation. The meaning of sexual freedom and its
connection with women's freedom is a subject which few
socialist writers have cared to broach. 'Socialist morality' in
the Soviet Union for a long time debarred serious discussion of
the subject within the world communist movement. Marx
himself – in this respect somewhat less liberal than Engels –
early in his life expressed traditional views on the matter:

... the sanctification of the sexual instinct through exclusivity, the
checking of instinct by laws, the moral beauty which makes nature's
commandment ideal in the form of an emotional bond – (this is) the
spiritual essence of marriage.[12]

Yet it is obvious that throughout history women have been
appropriated as sexual objects, as much as progenitors or
producers. Indeed, the sexual relationship can be assimilated
to the statute of possession much more easily and completely
than the productive or reproductive relationship. Contemporary sexual vocabulary bears eloquent witness to this – it is a
comprehensive lexicon of reification – 'bird, fruit, chick ...'
Later Marx was well aware of this: '*Marriage* ... is incontest-
ably a form of *exclusive private property*.'[13] But neither he nor
his successors ever tried seriously to envisage the implications
of this for socialism, or even for a structural analysis of
women's conditions. Communism, Marx stressed in the same
passage, would not mean mere 'communalization' of women
as common property. Beyond this, he never ventured.

Some historical considerations are in order here. For if
socialists have said nothing, the gap has been filled by liberal
ideologues. Fairly recently, in his book, *Eros Denied*, Wayland
Young argues that western civilization has been uniquely
repressive sexually, and, in a plea for greater sexual freedom

12. Karl Marx: 'Chapitre de Mariage', *Oeuvres Complètes,* ed. Molitor
Oeuvres Philosophiques, I, p. 25.

13. Karl Marx: *Private Property and Communism,* op. cit., p. 153.

today, compares it at some length with oriental and ancient societies. It is striking, however, that his book makes no reference whatever to women's status in these different societies, or to the different forms of marriage-contract prevalent in them. This makes the whole argument a purely formal exercise – an obverse of socialist discussions of women's position which ignore the problem of sexual freedom and its meanings. For while it is true that certain oriental or ancient (and indeed primitive) cultures were much less puritanical than western societies, it is absurd to regard this as a kind of 'transposable value' which can be abstracted from its social structure. In effect, in many of these societies sexual openness was accompanied by a form of polygamous exploitation which made it, in practice, an expression simply of masculine domination. Since art was the province of man, too, this freedom finds a natural and often powerful expression in art – which is often quoted as if it were evidence of the total quality of human relationships in the society. Nothing could be more misleading. What is necessary, rather than this naïve, hortatory core of historical example, is some account of the co-variation between the degrees of sexual liberty and openness, and the position and dignity of women in different societies.

Sexuality and the Position of Women:
Some Historical Examples

Some points are immediately obvious. The actual history is much more dialectical than any liberal account presents it. Unlimited juridical polygamy – whatever the sexualization of the culture which accompanies it – is clearly a total derogation of woman's autonomy, and constitutes an extreme form of oppression. Ancient China is a perfect illustration of this. A sensual culture and a society in which the father as head of the household wielded an extraordinary despotism. The Chinese paterfamilias was 'a liturgical (semi-official) policeman of his kin group'.[14] In the West, however, the advent of monogamy was in no sense an *absolute* improvement. It certainly did not

14. Karl Wittfogel: *Oriental Despotism*, 1957, p. 116.

create a one-to-one equality – far from it. Engels commented accurately:

> Monogamy does not by any means make its appearance in history as the reconciliation of man and woman, still less as the highest form of such a reconciliation. On the contrary, it appears as the subjugation of one sex by the other, as the proclamation of a conflict between the sexes entirely unknown hitherto in prehistoric times.[15]

But in the Christian era, monogamy took on a very specific form in the West. It was allied with an unprecedented regime of general sexual repression. In its Pauline version, this had a markedly anti-feminine bias, inherited from Judaism. With time this became diluted – feudal society, despite its subsequent reputation for asceticism, practised formal monogamy with considerable actual acceptance of polygamous behaviour, at least within the ruling class. But here again the extent of sexual freedom was only an index of masculine domination. In England, the truly major change occurred in the sixteenth century with the rise of militant puritanism and the increase of market relations in the economy. Lawrence Stone observes:

> In practice, if not in theory, the early sixteenth century nobility was a polygamous society, and some contrived to live with a succession of women despite the official prohibition on divorce.... But impressed by Calvinist criticisms of the double standard, in the late sixteenth century public opinion began to object to the open maintenance of a mistress.[16]

Capitalism and the attendant demands of the newly emergent bourgeoisie accorded woman a new status as wife and mother. Her legal rights improved; there was vigorous controversy over her social position: wife-beating was condemned. 'In a woman the bourgeois man is looking for a counterpart, not an equal.'[17] At the social periphery woman did occasionally achieve an equality which was more than her feminine function in a market society. In the extreme non-conformist sects

15. Friedrich Engels: op. cit., II, p. 224.
16. Lawrence Stone: *The Crisis of the Aristocracy,* 1965, pp. 663–4.
17. Simone de Beauvoir: *La Marche Longue,* 1957, trans. *The Long March,* 1958, p. 141.

women often had completely equal rights: the Quaker leader
Fox argued that the Redemption restored Prelapsarian equality
and Quaker women thereby gained a real autonomy. But
once most of the sects were institutionalized, the need for
family discipline was re-emphasized and woman's obedience
with it. As one historian, Keith Thomas, says, the Puritans
'had done something to raise women's status, but not really
very much'.[18] The patriarchal system was retained and maintained by the new economic mode of production – capitalism.
The transition to complete effective monogamy accompanied
the transition to modern bourgeois society as we know it
today. Like the capitalist market system itself, it represented a
historic advance, at great historic cost. The formal, juridical
equality of capitalist society and capitalist rationality now
applied as much to the marital as to the labour contract. In
both cases, nominal parity masks real exploitation and inequality. But in both cases the formal equality is itself a certain
progress, which can help to make possible a further advance.

Sexuality and the Position of Women: Today

The situation today is defined by a new contradiction. Once
formal conjugal equality (monogamy) is established, sexual
freedom as such – which under polygamous conditions was
usually a form of exploitation – becomes, conversely, a possible force for liberation. It then means, simply, the freedom of
both sexes to transcend the limits of present sexual institutions.

Historically, then, there has been a dialectical movement in
which sexual expression was 'sacrificed' in an epoch of more-
or-less puritan repression, which nevertheless produced a
greater parity of sexual roles and in turn creates the precondition for a genuine sexual liberation, in the dual sense of
equality *and* freedom – whose unity defines socialism.

18. Keith Thomas: *Women and the Civil War Sects*, Past and Present,
no. 13, 1958, p. 43.

Love and Marriage

This movement can be verified within the history of the 'sentiments'. The cult of *love* only emerges in the twelfth century in opposition to legal marital forms and with a heightened valorization of women (courtly love). It thereafter gradually became diffused, and assimilated to marriage as such, producing that absurdity – a *free* choice for *life*. What is striking here is that monogamy as an institution in the West, anticipated the idea of love by many centuries. The two have subsequently been officially harmonized, but the tension between them has never been abolished. There is a formal contradiction between the voluntary contractual character of 'marriage' and the spontaneous uncontrollable character of 'love' – the passion that is celebrated precisely for its involuntary force. The notion that it occurs only once in every life and can therefore be integrated into a voluntary contract, becomes decreasingly plausible in the light of everyday experience – once sexual repression as a psycho-ideological system becomes at all relaxed.

Obviously, the main breach in the traditional value-pattern has, so far, been the increase in premarital sexual experience. This is now virtually legitimized in contemporary society. But its implications are explosive for the ideological conception of marriage that dominates this society: that it is an exclusive and permanent bond. An American anthology, *The Family and the Sexual Revolution*, reveals this very clearly:

> As far as extra-marital relations are concerned, the anti-sexualists are still fighting a strong, if losing, battle. The very heart of the Judaeo-Christian sex ethic is that men and women shall remain virginal until marriage and that they shall be completely faithful after marriage. In regard to premarital chastity, this ethic seems clearly on the way out, and in many segments of the populace is more and more becoming a dead letter.[19]

The current wave of sexual liberalization, in the present context, *could* become conducive to the greater general free-

19. Albert Ellis: 'The Folklore of Sex', in *The Family and the Sexual Revolution*, ed. E. M. Schur, 1966, p. 35.

dom of women. Equally, it could presage new forms of oppression. The puritan-bourgeois creation of 'counterpart'
(not equal) has produced the *precondition* for emancipation. But
it gave statutory legal equality to the sexes at the cost of greatly
intensified repression. Subsequently – like private property
itself – it has become a brake on the further development of a
free sexuality. Capitalist market relations have historically
been a precondition of socialism; bourgeois marital relations
(contrary to the denunciation of the *Communist Manifesto*) may
equally be a precondition of women's liberation.

4. Socialization of Children

Woman's biological 'destiny' as mother becomes a cultural
vocation in her role as socializer of children. In bringing up
children, woman achieves her main social definition. Her
suitability for socialization springs from her physiological
condition: her ability to produce milk and occasional relative
inability to undertake strenuous work loads. It should be said
at the outset that suitability is not inevitability. Several
anthropologists make this clear. Lévi-Strauss writes:

In every human group, women give birth to children and take care
of them, and men rather have as their speciality hunting and warlike
activities. Even there, though, we have ambiguous cases: of course,
men never give birth to babies, but in many societies ... they are
made to act as if they did.[20]

Evans-Pritchard's description of the Nuer tribe depicts just
such a situation. Margaret Mead comments on the element of
wish-fulfilment in the assumption of a *natural* correlation of
feminity and nurturance:

We have assumed that because it is convenient for a mother to wish
to care for her child, this is a trait with which women have been
more generously endowed by a careful teleological process of
evolution. We have assumed that because men have hunted, an

20. Claude Lévi-Strauss: 'The Family', in *Man, Culture and Society*,
ed. H. L. Shapiro, 1956, p. 274.

activity requiring enterprise, bravery and initiative, they have been endowed with these useful attitudes as part of their sex-temperament.[21]

However, the cultural allocation of roles in bringing up children – and the limits of its variability – is not the essential problem for consideration. What is much more important is to analyse the nature of the socialization process itself and its requirements.

The sociologist, Talcott Parsons, in his detailed analysis claims that it is essential for the child to have two 'parents', one who plays an 'expressive' role, and one who plays an 'instrumental' role.[22] The nuclear family revolves around the two axes of generational hierarchy (parents and children), and of the two parental roles (mother-expressive and father-instrumental). The role division dervies from the mother's ability and the father's inability to breast-feed. In all groups, Parsons and his colleagues assert, even in those primitive tribes where the father appears to nurture the child (such as those discussed by Evans-Pritchard and Mead), the male plays the instrumental role *in relation* to the wife-mother. At one stage the mother plays an instrumental and expressive role *vis-à-vis* her infant: this is in the very first years when she is the source of approval and disapproval as well as of love and care. However, after this, the father, or male substitute (in matrilineal societies the mother's brother) takes over. In a modern industrial society two types of role are clearly important: the adult role in the family of procreation, and the adult occupational role in outside work. The function of the family as such reflects the function of the women within it; it is primarily expressive. The person playing the integrated-

21. Margaret Mead: 'Sex and Temperament', in *The Family and The Sexual Revolution*, op. cit., pp. 207-8.

22. Talcott Parsons and Robert F. Bales: *Family, Socialization and Interaction Process*, 1956, p. 47. 'The area of instrumental function concerns relations of the system to its situation outside the system ... and 'instrumentally' establishing the desired relations to *external* goal-objects. The expressive area concerns the 'internal' affairs of the system, the maintenance of integrative relations between the members, and regulation of the patterns and tension levels of its component units.'

adaptive-expressive role cannot be off all the time on in-strumental-occupational errands – hence there is a built-in inhibition of the woman's work outside the home. Parsons's analysis makes clear the exact role of the maternal socializer in contemporary American society.[23] It fails to go on to state that other aspects and modes of socialization are conceivable. What is valuable in Parsons' work is simply his insistence on the central importance of socialization as a process which is constitutive of any society (no Marxist has provided a comparable analysis). His general conclusion is that:

> It seems to be without serious qualification the opinion of com-petent personality psychologists that, though personalities differ greatly in their degrees of rigidity, certain broad fundamental patterns of 'character' are laid down in childhood (so far as they are not genetically inherited) and are not radically changed by adult experience. The exact degree to which this is the case or the exact age levels at which plasticity becomes greatly diminished, are not at issue here. The important thing is the fact of childhood character formation and its relative stability after that.[24]

Infancy

This seems indisputable: one of the great revolutions of modern psychology has been the discovery of the decisive specific weight of infancy in the course of an individual life – a psychic time disproportionately greater than the chronologi-cal time. Freud began the revolution with his work on infantile sexuality; Melanie Klein radicalized it with her work on the first year of the infant's life. The result is that today we know

23. One of Parsons' main theoretical innovations is his contention that what the child strives to internalize will vary with the content of the reciprocal role relationships in which he is a participant. R. D. Laing, in *Family and Individual Structure,* 1966, contends that a child may internalize an entire system – i.e. 'the family'.

24. Talcott Parsons: *The Social System,* 1952, p. 227. There is no doubt that the Women's Liberation Movement, with its practical and theoretical stress on the importance of child-care, has accorded the subject the seriousness it needs. See, for instance, 'Women's Liberation: Notes on Child-Care' produced by the Women's Centre, 36 West 22nd St, New York.

far more than ever before how delicate and precarious a process the passage from birth to childhood is for everyone. It would seem that the fate of the adult personality can be largely decided in the initial months of life. The preconditions for the later stability and integration demand an extraordinary degree of care and intelligence on the part of the adult who is socializing the child, as well as a persistence through time of the same person.

These undoubted advances in the scientific understanding of childhood have been widely used as an argument to reassert women's quintessential maternal function, at a time when the traditional family has seemed increasingly eroded. The psychologist, Bowlby, studying evacuee children in the Second World War, declared: 'essential for mental health is that the infant and young child should experience a warm, intimate, and continuous relationship with his mother,'[25] setting a trend which has become cumulative since. The emphasis of familial ideology has shifted from a cult of the biological ordeal of maternity (the pain which makes the child precious, etc.) to a celebration of mother-care as a social act. This can reach ludicrous extremes:

For the mother, breast-feeding becomes a complement to the act of creation. It gives her a heightened sense of fulfilment and allows her to participate in a relationship as close to perfection as any that a woman can hope to achieve. . . . The simple fact of giving birth, however, does not of itself fulfil this need and longing. . . . Motherliness is a way of life. It enables a woman to express her total self with the tender feelings, the protective attitudes, the encompassing love of the motherly woman.[26]

The tautologies, the mystifications, the sheer absurdities point to the gap between reality and ideology.

25. John Bowlby, cit. Bruno, Bettelheim: 'Does Communal Education Work? The Case of the Kibbutz', in *The Family and the Sexual Revolution,* op. cit., p. 295. These evacuee war children were probably suffering from more than mother-loss, e.g. bombings and air-raids?

26. Betty Ann Countrywoman: *Redbrook,* June, 1960, cit. Betty Friedan: *The Feminine Mystique,* Penguin, 1965, p. 51.

Family Patterns

This ideology corresponds in dislocated form to a real change in the pattern of the family. As the family has become smaller, each child has become more important; the actual *act* of reproduction occupies less and less time, and the socializing and nurturance process increase commensurately in significance. Contemporary society is obsessed by the physical, moral and sexual problems of childhood and adolescence. Ultimate responsibility for these is placed on the mother. Thus the mother's reproductive role has retreated as her socializing role has increased. In the 1890s in England a mother spent fifteen years in a state of pregnancy and lactation: in the 1960s she spent an average of four years. Compulsory schooling from the age of five, of course, reduces the maternal function very greatly after the initial vulnerable years.

The present situation is then one in which the qualitative importance of socialization during the early years of the child's life has acquired a much greater significance than in the past – while the quantitative amount of a mother's life spent either in gestation or child-rearing has greatly diminished. It follows that socialization cannot simply be elevated to the woman's new maternal vocation. Used as a mystique, it becomes an instrument of oppression. Moreover, there is no inherent reason why the biological and social mother should coincide. The process of socialization is, in itself, invariable – but the person of the socializer can vary. Observers of collective methods of child-rearing in the kibbutzim in Israel note that the child who is reared by a trained nurse (though normally maternally breast-fed) does not suffer the back-wash of typical parental anxieties and thus may positively gain by the system. This possibility should not be fetishized in its turn (Jean Baby, speaking of the post-four-year-old child, goes so far as to say that 'complete separation appears indispensable to guarantee the liberty of the child as well as the mother'.[27]) But what it does reveal is the viability of plural forms of

27. Jean Baby: *Un Monde Meilleur*, Maspero, 1964, p. 99.

socialization – neither necessarily tied to the nuclear family, nor to the biological parent, or rather to *one* of the biological parents – the mother.

Conclusion

The lesson of these reflections is that the liberation of women can only be achieved if *all four* structures in which they are integrated are transformed – Production, Reproduction, Sexuality and Socialization. A modification of any of them can be offset by a reinforcement of another (as increased socialization has made up for decreased reproduction). This means that a mere permutation of the form of exploitation is achieved. The history of the last sixty years provides ample evidence of this. In the early twentieth century, militant feminism in England and the U.S.A. surpassed the labour movement in its violence. The vote – a political right – was eventually won. None the less, though a simple completion of the formal legal equality of bourgeois society, it left the socio-economic situation of women virtually unchanged. The wider legacy of the suffrage was practically nil: the suffragettes, by and large, proved unable to move beyond their own initial demands, and many of their leading figures later became extreme reactionaries. The Russian Revolution produced a quite different experience. In the Soviet Union in the 1920s, advanced social legislation aimed at liberating women above all in the field of sexuality; divorce was made free and automatic for either partner, thus effectively liquidating marriage; illegitimacy was abolished, abortion was free, etc. The social and demographic effects of these laws in a backward, semi-literate society bent on rapid industrialization (needing, therefore, a high birthrate) were – predictably – catastrophic.[28] Stalinism soon produced a restoration of traditional iron norms. Inheritance was reinstated, divorce made inaccessible, abortion illegal, etc.

28. For a fuller account of this see Chapter IVA of Kate Millet's *Sexual Politics*, op. cit.

The State cannot exist without the family. Marriage is a positive value for the Socialist Soviet State only if the partners see in it a lifelong union. So-called free love is a bourgeois invention and has nothing in common with the principles of conduct of a Soviet citizen. Moreover, marriage receives its full value for the State only if there is progeny, and the consorts experience the highest happiness of parenthood.

From the official journal of the Commissariat of Justice in 1939,[29]

Women still retained the right and obligation to work, but because these gains had not been integrated into the earlier attempts to free sexuality and abolish the family no general liberation has occurred.

In China, today there is still another experience. At this stage of the revolution all the emphasis is being placed on liberating women in *production*. This has produced an impressive social promotion of women. But it seems to have been accompanied by a tremendous repression of sexuality and a rigorous puritanism (rampant in civic life). This corresponds not only to the need to mobilize women massively in economic life, but to a deep cultural reaction against the brutality, corruption and prostitution prevalent in Imperial and Kuo Ming Tang China (a phenomenon unlike anything in Czarist Russia). Because the exploitation of women was so great in the *ancien régime* women's participation at village level in the Chinese Revolution was uniquely high. As for reproduction, the Russian cult of maternity in the 1930s and 1940s has not been repeated for demographic reasons: indeed, China may be one of the first countries in the world to provide free State authorized contraception on a universal scale to the population. Again, however, given the low level of industrialization and fear produced by imperialist encirclement, no all-round advance could be expected.

Probably it is only in the highly developed societies of the West that an authentic liberation of women can be envisaged today. But for this to occur, there must be a transformation

29. *Sotsialisticheskaya Zakonnost,* 1939, no. 2, cit. N. Timasheff: 'The Attempt to Abolish the Family in Russia', in *The Family,* ed. N. W. Bell and E. F. Vogel, 1960, p. 59.

of *all* the structures into which they are integrated, and all the contradictions must coalesce, to explode – a *unité de rupture*. A revolutionary movement must base its analysis on the uneven development of each structure, and attack the weakest link in the combination. This may then become the point of departure for a general transformation. What is the situation of the different structures today? What is the concrete situation of the women in each of the positions in which they are inserted?

Chapter Six

The Position of Women: 2

I have taken the situation of women in England as a model.
The foregoing theoretical points are 'tight' and barely illustrated. This is both a factual and impressionistic account of
women at work (and the educational system that underpins
it), and of women in the home – their maternal, marital and
socializing roles and their sexual status.

These are the 'four structures' – Production, Reproduction,
Socialization, and Sexuality. I hope it will serve as amplifica-
tion and illustration.

Women in England

Production: The Work Situation

Sixty-eight per cent of the population of England is working-
class. Accordingly, the same percentage of women are
working-class; the majority of women are the wives and
daughters of working-class men, and the majority of them are
engaged in working-class work. Though, by the downward
mobility of women in marriage and by their upward mobility
in work, the picture is slightly blurred. There is a marginal
area where working-class women move up into secretarial,
clerical and general low-paid white-collar work. Here they
meet middle-class women, for whom these are normally the
only available jobs. But unlike in, say, America or Germany,
there has not been in England a vast increase of women in the
service sector. Most women work as un-skilled or semi-skilled
industrial labour, mainly in food, clothing, textiles, electrical

engineering, or, as clerical assistants, within the professional and scientific services and distributive trades.

The Equal Pay Act was passed in 1970. There are roughly nine million women in the work force and, twelve per cent of them receive equal pay. However, the concept of equal pay is highly problematic; it is usually presented in a way that is divisive of workers. As though the men who are working are somehow keeping the women who are working from getting the same rates. Ask many a woman whether she wants equal pay and the answer is likely to be 'no!' 'It wouldn't be fair, men do heavier work, we don't want to *take away* from their pay-packet, they are the bread-winners, we work for extras.' And men will give the same type of response. As though wages were geared to people's needs, and not to profits! The desultory efforts by the Trade Union Congress and specific unions to support equal pay and to counter this divisive presentation of the issue, stress that it is in the interest of all workers to urge its implementation because, among other reasons, in times of economic recession and forced labour redundancy (such as we are now entering), women form a pool of cheap labour. But women don't simply establish this threat: *they are a permanent sector of cheap labour. Ninety-five per cent of women do work only done by women. It is not 'equal' pay that is wanted: but more pay. Much more: to bring their pay up to the national male average means practically doubling women's wages.*

'Equal pay' suggesting, as it does, that working women should get a bigger share of working men's cake, merely underlines a whole position that divides the working class. With the new Act, when a pay rise is awarded in a mixed industry, women's pay is supposed to go up commensurately. It is a lot to ask men or women to keep down the claims of the entire work-force because the women's supplementary award will have to be deducted from the increase demanded. Because women are asked to fight for equal pay – and in ninety-five per cent of the cases there is no one for them to be equal to – they see themselves in a subsidiary role waiting to 'catch up' with the men, not pressing for increases simply because increases are what they ought to get and what male militants would have struck for long ago. On the whole 'equal pay' can now be tucked in as a legislative clause in a pay demand: it is not a rallying cry to militancy.

Women working with women, doing 'women's work', employed as cheap labour, seeing their wages as secondary, can have social, but not political solidarity amongst themselves. Their first economic concern (and hence their political one) is their husband's pay-packet. Women are notoriously presented as strike-breakers. If this is so, it is all too understandable. They cannot strike themselves because their work is not important anyway – a strike would assert that it was. In addition, the married ones are usually without social security in their own right and, poorly unionized, there is rarely strike pay available. Dependent on their men, they cannot afford to let them strike either. Sexual division at work (or into types of work) means that men and women cannot relate as workers: they relate as individual couples, dependent on each other, hence making demands on each other, not on the employers.

The major Post Office strike in England, January to March, 1971, highlights the situation: here were a union of men and women, an official strike, men and women largely doing different work. The press did its usual crowing over the high number of women telephonists who, despite the strike, clocked in for work. An appreciative 'public' sent the girls flowers. It makes depressing reading. These 'girls' either saw their work as a public service (secondary to that of their husbands; reared as helpmate precisely to serve, how else can they see it?), or, if they were single women in bedsitters, alone, how would they pay their rent? The conservative role of women (that is always being stressed by 'wait-till-after-the-revolution' male militants) is *not* theirs, but an intrinsic part of the sexually divided labour force and an economic system that enforces the unity of the couple rather than the solidarity of workers. An example: a friend of mine had a phone call from her sister, one of the flower-beshowered, noble, strike-breaking telephonists. She was in tears, her husband wouldn't let her strike (the family desperately needed her 'extra' money) and had, himself, driven her through the

lines of angry pickets, to work, to await the feelings of her
friends – the women who had struck.

Given, then, that the *family* structure dominates even at the
scene of work (or behind the scenes determines it), are instances like the following surprising?

All four hundred employees at the Typhoo Tea works, Birmingham,
went on unofficial strike yesterday because a forewoman repri-
manded a workman. A shop-steward said, 'The forewoman should
have referred any question of discipline to the man's foreman and
not acted as she did in speaking to the man.'[1]

Three hundred of the four hundred and seventy people who
struck over this breach of discipline were women. The man,
as head of the household, must preserve his status at work.

The trade-unions often merely echo the divisive element
built into the labour situation, a situation into which men and
women as individuals are trapped, but which one might hope
an organization ostensibly based on class-struggle would
attempt to counteract. Although 50 per cent of men are
unionized, the figure is only 25 per cent for women. This is
serious in a country in which until very recently, the working-
class struggle (in so far as it has existed) has largely been
through union activity. For many women – for instance
domestic workers – no union exists. No one has calculated
the number of women employed, at unbelievably exploitative
rates, in home-based jobs; envelope addressing, typing,
leafletting, knitting, 'finishing' from textile factories and so
on. They are outside the computed work-force. The T.U.C.
constantly urges the recruitment of new union members, but
what about the creation of new (or more inclusive) unions to
protect the ununionized? What about an all-out effort to
combat attitudes such as the following, which reads like a
parody of the divisive employment situation described above:

One old conference hand (male) assured me that women delegates
were still not taken quite seriously, especially at the T.U.C. Either
they got a special cheer for being delightfully feminine, or were
suffered because they were not.[2]

1. *Daily Telegraph,* 16 December 1963.
2. *Guardian,* 8 September 1966.

Women as ununionized cheap labour, pose a threat very comparable to that of immigrants:

Around 2,500 men went on strike yesterday because they fear a petticoat takeover at their factory. Strikers claimed that women – who earn £1.15.6d. a week less than men – had been given men's jobs on two automated assembly lines.

But the management of the works -- Britain's biggest disc brake factory – say that the jobs involved are women's work. 500 women disagreed and walked out with the strikers. ... Mr Bryn Richards, an Amalgamated Engineering Union official at the works, said: 'This could be the thin end of the wedge. With automation some firms might say that the whole factory could be run by women. We do not dispute that these jobs can be done by women. But because automation makes a job easier, there is no reason to take it from a man who has sweated over it for years and give it to a woman.'

A statement by the firm said their proposals were in the employees best interests because of the shortage of male labour.[3]

Cultural conservatism by *both sexes* compounds an economic system devised to make humanity prey on itself. Men are set against women by their own job insecurity. Only loyalty to traditions of feminine deference saves them. Courtesy unites, by its own hierarchies, what the economy divides.

The women machinists at Ford's (Dagenham) whose 1968 strike for equal pay was one of the mainsprings of Women's Liberation in England were, in fact, fighting for better female rates. This opened up the question of estimating the nature of the work done. Women's work is considered 'light' but, in fact, 'light' work (in particular automated jobs) imposes immense mental strain and physical fatigue. Recently, I talked with women in three factories, each with different types of work. The first, a biscuit factory was not automated. The second was a bacon factory which had mixed conventional and automated machinery, and the third was a foundry employing men and women in the same sheds.

The women in the biscuit factory spent as much as three hours a day travelling (time unpaid) in company buses from outlying districts as far as 40 miles distant. They were mostly

3. *Daily Herald,* 23 July 1964.

married with families. They worked a 42 hour week and took
home roughly £10 at the end of it. The conditions were early
industrial, reminding one of the heritage of being the first
industrial nation. The women stood in line simply packing
different shaped biscuits into different shaped boxes as they
came along the conveyor belt. I asked a foreman what he
would feel about doing the job. He replied: 'Oh, I've tried it,
so have a number of the foremen, so have those men there.'
He pointed to the Pakistanis sweeping the floor – the only
other men there. 'After twenty minutes we fall over. That's
the trouble with men, they want to see where something comes
from and where it's going. Now a woman, she's good, the
job doesn't matter to her, she's not interested, her hands
work, she chats to her neighbour but she doesn't look from
side to side as a man does. Consequently she doesn't get giddy
and fall over.' The women confirmed this difference. Talking
this over with friends afterwards, one said, 'But, of course,
weren't you brought up as a girl, to keep your eyes down
demurely, never to look to right nor left as you walked down
the street. Even now, can you sit in a café alone without a
book, looking round, staring as men do?' Does women's
social training fit them for monotonous work?

In the automated section of the bacon factory, the girls
were young. Indeed, it was found that they could rarely stand
the pace after the age of 27. They had five tea breaks on a
morning shift and despite this necessary concession still
suffered from serious headaches and eye-strain. I had both in
five minutes. It was like working at an op-art painting.
Brilliant metal bands zoomed down on you from right to left;
coming up to these in a rapid, pulsating movement were a
series of further shiny, interlocking metal strips, rising along a
vertical path; as these met, a luminous green marker showed
the weight of the bacon, right or wrong, to be measured and
corrected. At the end of the lines a vast scoreboard counted
the completed boxes. For every thousand, the women cheered.

In the foundry one saw the meaning of protective legislation
for women. All workers were paid piece-rates – the women
couldn't work overtime or nights, they couldn't lift heavy

weights (this restriction was constantly broken). In a job where equal pay was enforced they got the worst pieces and hence the lowest pay. And again social conditioning helped the profits and hindered the women. It was varied work (different tractor parts to be constructed or assembled). It was always the women who were moved from job to job. The foreman explained: 'Ask a man to shift and by the time he's finished arguing, the job could have been done; you see he wastes time and loses money by changing jobs. Now a woman, you can move her as much as you want and she'll never complain, she'll just get on with whatever she's told to do.' Seen but not heard.

Given that they see their work as subsidiary (and that it is seen and treated as such) how do women 'justify' it? Most women say they need the money for 'extras' and so it is classified in sociological surveys. 'Extras' usually turn out, on pressing, to be clothes for the children, household or family goods that could not otherwise be bought. Another frequent reason is the social company – the chats with other women. I was given this reason by one of the women working in the foundry. I was standing beside her, screaming above the din, my throat sore from a metal dust that was acknowledged to corrode paintwork. 'But how can you talk to each other?' 'We lip-read.'

The pattern for professional women in England is broadly the same as in other advanced capitalist countries. They either work in female dominated jobs (in which case, as in nursing and teaching, the whole profession is down-graded; its status equals a service, its money befits a 'charity') or they are such a minute percentage of the profession that they are isolated into that ironic category 'exceptional women'. Does this categorization raise the egos of their colleagues who are 'ordinary' men? Even the tiny crannies that women occupy are suitably feminine – as doctors they specialize in obstetrics and gynaecology, as lawyers in divorce and family law. Perhaps the most relevant comment comes from a survey of 142 women graduates working in eight different firms. All the women were asked what were their ambitions 'and even among the fifteen with first-class honours degrees, only two had specific ambitions for promotion, though an additional one did add, perhaps significantly, that her ambition had been killed long ago and now she was interested only in obtaining equal pay.'[4] And on the other side of the same coin: 'When managers were questioned closely about the kind of work women could do or could not do, it was found in the great majority of cases that a job mentioned by a manager in one firm as unsuitable for women was, in fact, being done by women in some other firm.'[5]

In working-class jobs, women are segregated into 'women's work'. In middle-class jobs, women are isolated in 'a man's world'. This crucial difference again separates women but this time along class lines. It is difficult for women with such totally different experiences, not just of their class, but of the organization of their jobs, to find common ground either as workers or as women without a Women's Movement which offers precisely this. Ironically, the structure of work in capitalist societies does seem to place men, whatever their class, in Lionel Tyger's much vaunted 'groups'.[6] But women, even where they are a band of women (in 'women's work' employment) are forced to relate not to each other, but along the line of the marital couple.

In the case of working-class women, it seems that the economy is determinate – they are largely vocationally educated for the locally available 'women's work' in factories or offices (though school training for homemaking and hopeful embourgeoisement is, of course, crucial). Indeed one report on the function of girls' training for work could comment – 'The gap between school-leaving and marriage may soon be so small that we shall no longer need to ask "what shall we do with the ordinary girl?".'[7] Risking a crude generalization, the

4. *New Society*, 17 September 1964.
5. ibid.
6. Lionel Tyger: *Men in Groups,* Random House, 1969.
7. Advisory Officer in the Youth Employment Service, London County Council.

job market in this case determines a large part of the education. But with middle-class girls the ideological structure is paramount and the economic secondary. Of course, in both cases the two are very interlocked. The attitudes of parents and teachers guide a middle-class girl, either out of the professions altogether or into certain 'proper' fields.

Education

Over one third of the schools in England are single-sex schools. This is a considerably lower proportion than that of a decade ago, but expediency not policy has directed the change. The higher the academic standard of education, the more likely is it to be segregated.

The 'exceptional' women who make it in a man's world are, therefore, most likely to have spent their childhood years being educated in sexually segregated schools. The 'ordinary'[8] girl is generally educated together with boys, only to find herself in women-only jobs. Her experience of growing up with boys is, therefore, of use to her only in her home situation. Contrarily, the academic girl is liable to meet boys only in her social life (if then), not in her educational life, and then finds herself massively outnumbered by them at university and in her career. In this case neither sex has learnt to treat the other as serious work companions. This does not handicap the men who dominate the profession and can relate among themselves to their project, but it severely isolates the 'exceptional' woman, putting intolerable pressures on her to conform to masculine requirements in her production and to feminine standards in her manners. It also can make her fear to associate herself with other women as this would thus 'down-

8. 'Ordinary' and 'exceptional' are those mystified terms prevalent everywhere, but paramount in educational surveys, which are standard for children with low or high opportunity chances; one would guess that in the great majority of the cases they equal working-class and middle-to-upper class. The exceptions would be those 6 per cent of working-class children – in a country where they are 68 per cent of the population – who manage to get to university (see R. Titmuss: *Commitment to Welfare*, 1968 p. 32).

grade' her seriousness. The pattern is familiar in journalists and Members of Parliament who fight shy of 'women's issues' in order to keep their place in a man's world.

The effects on inter-sexual relations (private or public) of sexual segregation at school are hard to define precisely, but they are clearly of enormous importance. Easier to chart is the sexual discrimination within an educational system purporting to be equal. This discrimination, masked as 'differentiation', pertains in mixed and segregated schools. It is a combination of attitudes that devalue a girl's achievement, and of a concrete lack of opportunities that determine it. For in following the trajectory of girls' education one thing, above all, emerges with crystal clarity. It is that there is no coincidence between the natural ability and intelligence of girls and the social devaluation they progressively undergo.

The vast majority of children change from junior school to secondary at eleven. The type of school they go to or the 'stream' or section within a school, is determined on ability – tested by examination or assessed by the teacher. The majority of children leave school at fifteen (with or without leaving examinations): those that stay on take first the Ordinary Level General Certificate of Education at sixteen, then the Advanced, at eighteen, and then leave possibly for higher education – University, Colleges of Education, Art, or Technology. At each point of measurement, eleven, sixteen and eighteen, girls perform marginally better than boys; but the direction of their achievement is different and, from the point of view of status and economic prestige, inferior. The range of subjects that girls take at 'Ordinary' level is narrower. More boys than girls stay on beyond the legally required leaving age, so that by eighteen, girls take only half as many 'Advanced' level papers as boys, and boys who are still at school outnumber the girls by two to one. By the time they get to university, women are only a quarter of the student body. Fewer apply for entrance, but also fewer succeed. With the exception of one or two of the newest universities none has a policy of sexual parity. Furthermore, the ratios of men and women will vary greatly according to the type of university. The decline in the percentage of women becomes sharper as the prestige of the university is higher. At the small civic university women are roughly 35 per cent of the students; at the larger civic university 25 per cent. But at Oxford and Cambridge they are only 12½ per cent. Post-graduate work sees the final step in the narrowing process between the sexes – 22 per cent of post-graduates are women, but if we exclude those who are qualifying for teaching with Diplomas of Education, the figure is only 14 per cent.

In academic subjects at secondary school and in institutions of higher education, a girl's career is a downhill struggle, a denial of her potentialities. The system is one of progressively contracting opportunity. The social climate and social order determine the attitudes of parents, teachers and girls alike in such a way as to offer an increasingly confined future. And even within this a more invidious 'differentiation' occurs. In principle, for boys and girls, there is no distinction in the type of academic subject studied. In practice there is an ominous difference visible in examination subjects. Less than two thirds as many girls as boys take sciences, and less than half as many take maths. The science that the girls do take is biology rather than physics and chemistry, thus apparently indicating a preference (whose?) for the human and tangible as opposed to the abstract and theoretical. By the time of university, only 2 per cent of those few women in science faculties will be taking applied science, over half, biology. Everywhere girls are discouraged from being scientific; in segregated schools they are given inadequate teaching and equipment for science. Teaching is largely a feminine profession, what the girl is not taught she can hardly teach to others. This absence from scientific subjects means, furthermore, that the relative position of girls' education is likely to deteriorate still further. The reason is simple, and directly linked to the fencing in of the girls' abilities. The current expansion of higher education is overwhelmingly in science and technology (by 1980 a 7 per cent proportional increase in universities alone, while the proportion in arts decreases). In future, therefore, girls will gain an even smaller share of university places than they do at present.

Already, the percentage of girls studying science is smaller than before the war. In addition, the Colleges of Advanced Technology are the focal point of the overwhelming increase in higher education. Ninety-five per cent of all full-time students in Colleges of Advanced Technology are in science or technology: around 80 per cent of the entrants are men.

> ... A boy is usually excited by the prospect of a science course. ... He experiences a sense of wonder and a sense of power. ... He comes readily to his teacher hoping to learn *how to control events*. ... The girl may come to the science lesson with a less eager curiosity than the boy, but she too will need to *feel at home* with machinery and *will be subject to the prestige* which science has in the world . . .[9]

(My italics)

No comment ...

These words are from the Newsom Report, the Government Commission that defined the type of schooling suitable for the non-academic child – roughly two thirds of the school-age population – these are the children relegated to Secondary Modern schools or the lower reaches of Comprehensives. The Report indicates the aims and function of such education with great clarity. They are: 'Practical, realistic, vocational, choice.' The boy is most likely to be trained for mechanical work. The Report remarks:

> It would seem wholly sensible to plan courses for some of these boys centring round the use, perhaps the making, of tools, the handling and working of various types of materials; the operating and maintenance of machines. Such work could be realistic in relating its materials and examples to the dominant industries of the area; although a school would need to watch that it did not over-produce hopeful candidates for non-existent vacancies.[10]

The girl, on the other hand, is likely to go on to work in an office, a shop, the catering trade, the clothing industry or other light manufacturing trades. The authors of this seminal report think that these various occupations 'can all provide

9. *Half Our Future*, HMSO, 1963, p. 142. Referred to as 'The Newsom Report'. Statistics on higher education are taken from the Robbins Report, HMSO, 1963.

10. ibid., p. 36.

the material for courses at more than one level of ability'. The two-way process of training the child for a working- or lower-middle class occupation and of deriving an education from this work, is made explicit in, for instance, their comment on shorthand: 'It is extremely difficult to extract from shorthand, unlike many of the other craft skills which may be practised in vocational courses, any general educational content or applications beyond itself.'[11]

But where boys will have one occupation, girls have two. They are trained to *do* something – currently 'female' work – (secretarial or factory) and educated to *be* someone – a wife and mother. The same word, Ivocation' is used indifferently of both: 'To girls especially the personal aspect of vocation to marriage is already apparent. The interest is ready-made: there is an opportunity to give it depth of meaning.'[12] And Kathleen Ollerenshaw, one of the Report's committee, in her earlier book *Education for Girls*, wrote 'The incentive for girls to equip themselves for marriage and home-making is genetic.'[13] The fact that there is plenty of evidence to suggest that far from domestic work being a *natural* choice for a girl, it is often a burden already felt too heavily in her home, is callously commented on:

There may be some girls who are far from enthusiastic, because they have had their fill of scrubbing and washing-up and getting meals for the family at home; and yet, they may need all the more the education a good school course can give in the wider aspects of home-making, and the skills which will reduce the element of domestic drudgery.[14]

And Ollerenshaw, recording the complaint of one school girl, that she would prefer to spend her time on maths and science, not on domestic work, makes the inimitable comment: 'It is only fair to remark that this criticism must arise from old-fashioned teaching of domestic subjects.'[15]

11. ibid., p. 37.
12. ibid., p. 116.
13. Kathleen Ollerenshaw: *Education for Girls*, 1961, p. 186.
14. *Half our Future*, op. cit., p. 135.
15. *Education for Girls*, op. cit., p. 24.

In this non-academic type of education, roughly two out of five days are spent on practical subjects: arts, crafts and domestic subjects and typing for girls; metalwork, technical drawing, construction for boys. The two sexes are being classified as occupationally distinct groups.

Academic potential is largely assessed at eleven, these children – of both sexes – 'failed'. Much is done here, too, to suggest that getting a worse deal merely indicates that you are 'different'. These are negative children, their past is irrelevant. In what capacities they might not have been found wanting was never discussed. Child, parent, and teacher must look to the future (the 'suitable' adult work) and the *given* future be made to appear the result of choice where, in fact, it is a determinant of past education.

Education in England is structured along class lines. But, as at work, within their class possibilities, women have a special role – an oppressed one. The problem is the unity of women as an oppressed group across the class lines that are there to divide them. The 'privileged', middle- and upper-class woman who gets to university has never *seen* how under-privileged she is – she has been educated separately from her male equivalent. The working-class girl cannot see that she is any worse off than the boy – for both school and work are probably a nightmare. Indeed, she may even feel lucky, because one of her 'vocations', marriage, is presented as offering an 'escape'. For it is here that the ideology of freedom and choice is most prevalent: you don't choose to go to school, the notion that you choose your job has probably worn a bit thin, ah, but love and marriage ... the individual surges forth in final affirmation of herself (or himself), spontaneity breaks the walls of compulsion, a light from within and without shines through the greyness. ... The greatest number of boys and girls marry within a neighbourhood, and despite the downward mobility of girls the majority marry someone in their own social class.[16]

16. For a detailed account of 'mate-selection' habits, see Rosser and Harris: *The Family and Social Change*, 1965. Their survey is of Swansea, but is probably indicative of national trends.

Marriage and Motherhood

Most girls work full-time until their early twenties: either
leaving school at fifteen, marrying probably three to four
years later and having the first child at twenty-one, or staying
at school, then college, marrying and having a first child in
their mid-twenties. For the majority of women the pattern
goes roughly as follows: a few years at work, a few years as a
mother of young children at home,[17] back to work, maybe
sporadically, probably part-time till the children contribute
to the family income or till the husband retires and you both
live on a married couple's old-age pension: for the middle-
class woman – a few years' training, a few years' work, more
time as a mother of young and growing children – back to
work when the children leave home and are no longer economically dependent. Women who do not go out to work for
any noticeable period (full or part-time) after having children
fall into two opposite groups: the very poor, unsupported
mothers, or mothers of large low-income families on the one
hand, and on the other, non-professional, small family, middle-
class women, usually with slight (or non-existent) higher
educational background. It is this last group whose life forms
the magic mother-and-housewife image. First coming into
prominence as a socially significant phenomenon in the 1870s,
married women of leisure were a symptom and then a symbol
of prosperity. An idle wife meant the family could afford to
leave the hangover of feudal housewifery (e.g. the *production*
of food) to others, first to servants, later to shops and gadgets,
and certainly had no economic need for her to be in gainful
outside employment. The full-time housewife still bears this
significance: 'There's no need for *my* wife to work', 'I wouldn't
let my wife work', are ways of saying 'I'm doing alright' in
economic and job status. Like the long-grown little finger-
nail of the peasant turned petty-bourgeois shop-keeper,
artisan or small landlord, this housewife says, 'My man has

17. For a subjective account of the experience of being a mother of
young children see *The Politics of Housework*, Peckham Rye Women's
Liberation, published by Agitprop, 1970.

made it.' These are the women of the feminine mystique:
bridge-playing, charitable social work, endless clean sheets.
There are not very many of them. For most women, whether
working in the home or outside it, housework is an arduous
job, taking between seventy and one hundred hours a week.
The labour-saving gadgets of the feminine mystique are
elusive: the usual home washing-machine in Britain does not
do the washing for you (only the most expensive models do
this), the average refrigerator is still so small as virtually to
necessitate daily shopping for a family, the vacuum cleaner
heavy, and a great many households do not have even these
gadgets. The prevalent nineteenth-century house is more
staircase than rooms, central heating is rare, coal fires still
common, canned, frozen and pre-packed food, two to six
times as expensive as the root vegetables that need scrubbing
or peeling. Twenty-two per cent of households have totally
inadequate supplies of hot and cold water; over 18 per cent
have neither indoor toilet nor fixed washbasins; 40 per cent
have no refrigerator. And this is a welfare state with a low
poverty rating ... a 'consumer society'. The House of Pride
is indeed built on the sands of poverty: it is women who stand
with their feet in the sand struggling to make the appearance
of the home something to be proud of.

Some Implications

A survey of earnings in one sample week (in September, 1968)
revealed the following: 90.6 per cent of male manual workers,
95.4 per cent of male non-manual workers, 13.8 *per cent of
female manual workers* and 44.5 per cent of female non-manual
workers earned £15 and over.[18] Well over one third of women
at work are 'female manual workers'. What is crucial is not
that a woman's getting little over half a man's pay is 'unequal',
'unfair', it is that she *does not get a living wage*. The plight of the
unsupported mother is acute – that of the single woman
serious enough. One in five single women have to support a

18. *Employment and Productivity Gazette*, May, 1969.

dependant; of single men it is only one in eight who do so.

Women are brought up to think of themselves primarily as mothers and wives; yet finding themselves despite this, nevertheless out at work, it is this family identification that determines their relationship to their job and their companions. The dependence of the woman on the family and its dependence on her is an ideological and economic one. It is its pattern of relationships that she bears with her wherever she goes. Her husband's job is in all senses the most important, everything must give way to this. So that, working as she does with women, these companions are bound to be 'social' life. 'I like the company', 'we have a good giggle and a chat' sum up the predicament: work as a housewife isn't work – its 'being at home' (the place of leisure), work in the office or the factory isn't work – it's 'getting out of the house for a bit'. Working at home she is isolated, working outside the home she is enjoying some social life. There is no possibility here of comradeship or unity in struggle – the relationship of women workers is simply the counterpart of the loneliness of the home, it is a friendliness or its opposite. Because the economic role of women is obscured (its cheapness obscures it) women workers do not have the preconditions of class-consciousness. Their exploitation is invisible behind an ideology that masks the fact that they work at all – their work appears inessential. Furthermore, women's work is seen so often, not in economic terms at all, but in psychological: what she *needs* ('it's good for her to get out a bit'), what she can manage, and so on. Psychological analyses are always individual: the woman's isolation is reinforced by being compounded with her perpetual individualism. Cut off from other women at home, going to work 'for the company' she yet brings – at times of crisis – the isolation of the family to bear on the collective possibilities of the work situation, she does not have even a divided loyalty, for where dependence is intrinsic to the situation, loyalty is redundant.

Separated from her work companions by her dependence on her family, within this family she experiences a yet more fundamental division: that of herself and her husband – the original unity. A recent legal case epitomizes the matter: a judge has awarded a husband suffering from the death of his wife, a sum based on loss of her 'services', 10s. 0d. (50p) an hour. Ten shillings per hour for an estimated twenty hours a week housework – both figures illustrate the divorce of the legal system from the realities of daily living. Most women earn only 5s. 0d. (25p) per hour in outside employment and the majority of housewives work over three times as long as the suggested figure. Neither the husband nor anyone ever paid for those services in her lifetime, and, if previously he maintained her, now she is dead he doesn't, so maintenance can't cost very much or the judge would have deducted this sum. If, hypothetically, the wife had claimed for her husband's loss, it would have been as the loss of the 'breadwinner', a far higher sum. This division between the roles of man and wife is not simply a 'division of labour', it is the denigration of the one job to service and the elevation of the other to 'production'. A division – like all divisions – predicated on inequality.

Divided, individuated, isolated – a woman is yet, paradoxically, subjected to the most homogenizing, the most unindividual of ideologies – the nature of her so-called 'womanhood', 'feminity'. 'Women are alike the world over', 'Just like a woman', 'Oh women . . .'

Sexuality

The so-called 'sexual revolution' and the cult of libertarianism have probably permeated further in England than in the other countries of Women's Liberation. Among students and the young professional groups there is a renunciation of marriage not to be found in America where urban violence and loneliness seem to preserve a need for the institution. This renunciation means something different from that found amongst comparable groups who have done so for a long time in Sweden or Denmark. It is hard to define this difference. To me, it is perhaps best expressed as a quality of seriousness. Un-marriage, with or without children, in Sweden and Denmark is not a glamorous option – it is simply an option which may seem the right one. In England this unconventionality was established as a convention by pop and film stars (many of whom subsequently reneged); it is rarely an ideological commitment beyond the trendy one of gathering whatever rosebuds you may, or doing as your friends do. Clearly the youth cult and prevalence of the Hippy communities is far greater and stronger in America than anywhere else, but these are extrinsic and counter-social on every level: sex, drugs, violence, social organization, etc.... Their *mores* are less extreme but also more widespread in England, where drop-outs easily drop back in – an influence which works both ways. The most visible symptom of this is dress and personal appearance: it is not just in London's King's Road that the 'right' anything or nothing goes. It is as hard *not* to keep up with the changing (and multiple) fashions as it is to keep up with them. Beauty is all, in this epoch of loving and expansive narcissism. The commercial 'exploitation' (which comes first?) of this is phenomenal. The ex-Empire (or its remains) has been re-raided to reproduce itself in miniature concentration in Oxford Street: you can eat, dress and adorn – Indian, old Chinese, Arabian, African. ... And having been offered all possibilities for self-glorification, having produced the sexually radiant you, the commercial dimension of capitalism can re-use you; this time you, yourself, will do to sell the drabber products: cars, washing machines, life insurance. No city in the world boasts such a density of 'sexual objectification' on its bill-boards and subway ads, as does London.

It is this latter use of sexuality that Women's Liberation objects to – its 'consumption'. But what of its production in the first place? The vivacious sensuality encountered in England is certainly invigorating after the prevalent 'secondary' narcissism of North America where the passive 'health' of the body seems more urgent than its vitality. Multi-coloured and multi-shaped dresses are more enlivening than multi-coloured and multi-shaped vitamin pills on the breakfast table.

In the contradiction between its active production and

passive consumption, lies the potential strength of the 'sexual revolution'. For its production can burst its banks; individuals can discover a certain degree of real liberation in this sole enclave where self-expansion is admitted. Its potentially freeing effect lies in the stress between the genuine unorthodoxy it creates and the new orthodoxy it tries to establish. But, in the first place, it is only a potentiality; for this is a contradiction as yet unexplored. And, in the second, even if this were realized, it is only one aspect of the problem and might not have even a catalytic effect on the others.

For women, as to a lesser extent for men, the 'sexual revolution' has meant a positive increase in the amount of their sexual (and hence social) freedom; it has also meant an increase in their 'use' as sexual objects. The tension produced by the inevitable consequence of the one on the other has, in itself, been a motivating force behind the creation of a Women's Liberation Movement.[19] Illusorily offered the free and glorious expression of ourselves, it turned out to be only for a further alienation: turning ourselves into products which are then confiscated for use in a consumer society.

The position of women in England today offers an interesting model. The numerous contradictions (on various levels) are fairly apparent. Here, very clearly, women find themselves at both ends of the scale: the most 'primitive' and the most 'advanced'. Much of the work (and conditions of work) that women do in England is symptomatic of early capitalist societies. It is not just that they are in those industries which produce the most basic goods – the industries which replaced the feudal home – clothes and food; the fact is, that, as perpetual cheap labour, they are still vulnerable to the type of utilization described in the case of women travelling eighty miles to and from work; that as unacknowledged workers, in the home, they can provide a concealed labour force of home-

19. Conservative opponents of Women's Liberation contend that all women in it are ugly and hard up for a man, in other words, 'envious bitches'. Socialist opponents, with their puritanical traditions, claim that we are all young, pretty and middle-class, in other words, 'unserious'. Whatever the case, the conflict described above applies, and protest against it is valid.

based production. At the other end they are the subject of the
most advanced ideological utilization made by late capitalism;
its chief ideological means of creating its markets. Of course,
this overall contradiction is not in itself experienced as such,
but aspects of it are.

I stressed the quantity and hard work of housework, all of
which is true. But we must also not forget that this is counterposed against the slogan that 'housework is nothing'. No
ideological statement of this sort can afford to be completely
vacuous. In one sense, for, say, the American housewife in an
urban apartment with launderette in the basement, shopping
delivered, pre-prepared food, a large freezer, children at
school, etc. – it *is* nothing, (except that it is always there – you
never get away from it). I stressed the inferior education girls
in England receive, but this must be counterposed against the
invariable belief that 'education is equal'. Again, in a sense,
this is true for some. Most women are not short of education
– they have got more than enough for anything they are likely
to have the opportunity to do with it. In the home, and in
their educational acquisitions, women are *redundant*. They are
an invisible, primitive economic base, yet their services in a
technological world seem totally unnecessary. Of course, this
contradiction is obscured by the class division that separates
the extremes; as working-class women tend to occupy one end
of the scale and middle-class the other it is rarely embodied
in one individual. But this is the way the capitalist system uses
the class barrier, the privileges of the middle class gain a
stranglehold over all: women in both classes are oppressed by
an ideology that tells the working woman she is not working
and the more leisured woman that she was never meant to
anyway.

Advanced capitalist society is not homogeneous. The contradiction that women experience of being in the most 'primitive' and the most 'advanced' aspects of capitalist society,
(and the contradictions inherent *within* these aspects) came to a
head with the nature of the development of the latter in the
1960s. It may well be one of the reasons why it was at this
moment that a Women's Liberation Movement arose.

Chapter Seven

The Position of Women: 3

Some General Conclusions

(1) Production

Today, automation promises the *technical* possibility of abolishing completely the physical differential between man and woman in production. But under capitalist relations of production, the *social* possibility of this abolition is permanently threatened, and can easily be turned into its opposite, the actual diminution of woman's role in production as the labour force contracts.

This concerns the future; for the present the main fact to register is that woman's role in production is virtually stationary, and has been so for a long time now. In England in 1911, 30 per cent of the work-force were women; in 1970, 37 per cent. The composition of their jobs has not changed decisively either. The jobs are very rarely 'careers'; when they are not in the lowest positions on the factory-floor they are normally white-collar auxiliary positions (such as secretaries) – supportive to masculine roles. They are often jobs with a high 'expressive' content, such as 'service' tasks. Sociologists can put it bluntly: 'Within the occupational organization they are analogous to the wife-mother role in the family.'[1] The educational system underpins this role-structure. Seventy-five per cent of eighteen-year-old girls in England are receiving neither training nor education today. The pattern of 'instrumental' father and 'expressive' mother is not substantially changed when the woman is gainfully employed, as her job tends to be inferior to that of the man's, to which the family adapts. Thus, in all essentials, work – of the amount and type

1. Parsons and Bales: op. cit., p. 15n.

effectively available today – has not proved a salvation for women, quite the contrary.

(2) Reproduction

Scientific advance in contraception could, as we have seen, make involuntary reproduction – which accounts for the vast majority of births in the world today, and for a major proportion even in the West – a phenomenon of the past. But oral contraception – which has so far been developed in a form which exactly repeats the sexual inequality of Western society – is only at its beginnings. It is inadequately distributed across classes and countries and awaits further technical improvements. Its main initial impact is, in the advanced countries, likely to be psychological – it will certainly free women's sexual experience from many of the anxieties and inhibitions which have always afflicted it.[2] It will definitely divorce sexuality from procreation as a necessary complement.

The demographic pattern of reproduction in the West may or may not be widely affected by oral contraception. One of the most striking phenomena of recent years in the United States has been the sudden increase in the birth-rate. In the last decade it has been higher than that of under-developed countries such as India, Pakistan and Burma. In fact, this probably reflects simply the lesser economic burden of a large family in the richest country in the world. But it also reflects the magnification of familial ideology as a social force.

(3) Socialization

The changes in the composition of the work-force, the size of the family, the structure of education, and other factors – however limited from an ideal standpoint – have undoubtedly diminished the social function and importance of the family.

2. Jean Baby records the results of an inquiry carried out into attitudes to marriage, contraception and abortion of 3,191 women in Czechoslovakia in 1959: 80 per cent of the women had limited sexual satisfaction because of fear of conception, op. cit., p. 82n.

As an organization it is not a significant unit in the political power system, it plays little part in economic production and it is rarely the sole agency of integration into the larger society; thus at the macroscopic level it serves very little purpose.

The result has been a major displacement of emphasis on to the family's psycho-social function, for the infant and for the couple.[3] I have discussed the vital nucleus of truth in the emphasis on socialization of the child. It is essential that it is acknowledged and integrated entirely into any programme for the liberation of women. It is noticeable that it was one of the first concerns of the Women's Liberation Movement. Yet there is no doubt that the need for permanent, intelligent care of children in the initial three or four years of their lives can (and has been) exploited ideologically to perpetuate the family as a total unit, when its other functions have been visibly declining. Indeed, the attempt to focus women's existence exclusively on bringing up children, is manifestly harmful to children as well. Socialization is an exceptionally delicate process which requires a serene and mature socializer – a type which the frustrations of a *purely* family role are not liable to produce. Exclusive maternity is often in this sense 'counter-productive'. The mother discharges her own frustrations and anxieties in a fixation on the child. An increased awareness of the critical importance of socialization, far from leading to a restitution of classical maternal roles, should lead to a reconsideration of them – of what makes a good socializing agent who can genuinely provide security and stability for the child.

The same arguments apply with added force to the psycho-social role of the family for the couple. The belief that the family provides an impregnable enclave of intimacy and security in an atomized and chaotic cosmos assumes the absurd – that the family can be isolated from the community, and that its internal relationships will not reproduce in their own terms the external relationships which dominate the

3. See Berger and Kellner: 'Marriage and the Construction of Reality', *Diogenes,* Summer, 1964, for analyses of marriage and parenthood 'nomic-building' structure.

society. The family as a refuge from society in fact becomes a reflection of it.

(4) Sexuality

The major structure which at present is in rapid evolution is sexuality. Production, reproduction, and socialization are all more or less stationary in the West today in that they have not changed for three or more decades. Sexual repression, on the contrary, is proving less and less successful in regulating spontaneous behaviour. Marriage in its classical form is increasingly threatened by the liberalization of relationships before and after it which affects all classes today. In this sense, it is evidently the weak link in the chain – the particular structure that is the site of the most contradictions. I have already emphasized the progressive potential of these contradictions. In a context of juridical equality, the liberation of sexual experience from relations which are extraneous to it – whether procreation or property – could lead to true intersexual freedom. But it could also lead simply to new forms of neo-capitalist ideology and practice. For one of the forces behind the current acceleration of sexual freedom has undoubtedly been the conversion of contemporary capitalism from a production-and-work ethos to a consumption-and-fun ethos. This was already commented on in the early fifties.

… there is not only a growth of leisure, but work itself becomes both less interesting and less demanding for many … more than before, as job-mindedness declines, sex permeates the daytime as well as the playtime consciousness. It is viewed as a consumption good not only by the old leisure class, but by the modern leisure masses.[4]

The gist of Riesman's argument is that in a society bored by work, sex is the only activity, the only reminder of one's energies, the only competitive act; the last defence against *vis inertiae*. The same insight can be found, with greater theoretical depth, in Marcuse's notion of 'repressive de-sublimation'

4. Riesman: *The Lonely Crowd*, 1950, p. 154.

– the freeing of sexuality for its own frustration in the service of a coordinated and drugged social machine.[5] Society at present can well afford a play area of premarital *non*-procreative sexuality. Even marriage can save itself by increasing divorce and remarriage rates, signifying the importance of the institution itself. These considerations make it clear that sexuality, while it could contain the potential for liberation – can equally well be organized against any increase of its human possibilities. The new forms of reification and the commercial consumption of sexuality may void sexual freedom of any meaning. This is a reminder that while one structure may be the *weak link* in a unity like that of woman's condition, there can never be a solution through it alone.

What, then, is a possible revolutionary attitude? It must include both immediate and fundamental demands, in a single critique of the *whole* of women's situation, that does not fetishize any dimension of it. Modern industrial development, as has been seen, tends towards the separating out of the originally unified function of the family – procreation, socialization, economic subsistence, etc. – even if this 'structural differentiation' has been checked and disguised by the maintenance of a powerful family ideology.

In practical terms this means a coherent system of demands. The four elements of women's condition cannot merely be considered each in isolation; they form a structure of specific inter-relations. The contemporary family can be seen as a triptych of sexual, reproductive and socializatory functions (the woman's world) embraced by production (the man's world) – precisely a structure which in the final instance is determined by the economy. The exclusion of women from production – social human activity – and their confinement to a monolithic condensation of functions within a unity – the family – which is precisely unified in the *natural part* of each function, is the root cause of the contemporary *social* definition of women as *natural* beings. Any emancipation movement must still concentrate on the economic element – the entry of

5. See Marcuse: *Eros and Civilization*, Routledge, 1956 and Reimut Reiche: *Sexuality and Class Struggle*, New Left Books, 1970.

women fully into public industry and *the right to earn a living wage*. The error of the old socialists was to see the other elements as reducible to the economic; hence the call for the entry of women into production was accompanied by the purely abstract slogan of the abolition of the family. Economic demands must be accompanied by coherent policies for the other three elements; policies which at particular junctures may take over the primary role in immediate action.

Economically, the most elementary demand is not the right to work or receive equal pay for work – the two traditional demands – but *the right to equal work itself*. At present, women perform unskilled, uncreative, service jobs that can be regarded as 'extensions' of their expressive familial role. They are overwhelmingly waitresses, office-cleaners, hair-dressers, clerks, typists. In the working class, occupational mobility is thus sometimes easier for girls than for boys – they can enter the white-collar sector at a lower level. But only two in a hundred women are in administrative or managerial jobs, and less than five in a thousand are in the professions. Women are poorly unionized and receive far less money than men for the manual work they perform: this, among other things, represents a massive increment of exploitation for the employer.

Education

The whole pyramid of economic discrimination rests on a solid extra-economic foundation – education. The demand for equal work, in Britain, should also take the form of a demand for an *equal educational system*. In post-compulsory education there is no evidence whatever of progress. The proportion of girl university students is the same as it was in the 1920s. Until these injustices are ended, there is no chance of equal work for women. It goes without saying that the content of the educational system, which actually instils limitation of aspiration in girls, needs to be changed as much as methods of selection.

Only if it is founded on equality can production be truly differentiated from reproduction and the family; and the wo-

man at work not bear with her the attitudes of the home. But
this in turn requires a whole set of non-economic demands as a
complement. Reproduction, sexuality, and socialization also
need to be free from coercive forms of unification. Traditionally, the socialist movement has called for the 'abolition
of the bourgeois family'. This slogan must be rejected as
incorrect today. It is maximalist in the bad sense, posing a
demand which is merely a negation without any coherent
construction subsequent to it. The reasons for the historic
weakness of the notion is that the family was never analysed
structurally – in terms of its different functions. It was a
hypostatized entity – just like its ideology in contemporary
society. The abstraction of its abolition corresponds to the
abstraction of its conception. The strategic concern is the
liberation of women and the equality of the sexes, not the
abolition of the family. The consequences of this demand are
no less radical, but they are concrete and positive, and can be
integrated into the real course of history. The family, as it
exists at present is, in fact, incompatible with either women's
liberation or the equality of the sexes. But equality will not
come from its administrative abolition, but from the historical
differentiation of its functions. The revolutionary demand
should be for the liberation of these functions from an oppressive monolithic fusion. This dissociation of reproduction
from sexuality, frees sexuality from alienation in unwanted
reproduction (and fear of it), and reproduction from subjugation to chance and uncontrollable causality. It is thus an
elementary demand to press for free State provision for oral
contraception. The straightforward abolition of illegitimacy
as a legal notion as in Sweden and Russia has a similar im-
plication; it would separate marriage civicly from parenthood.

The problem of socialization poses more difficult questions,
as has been seen. But the need for intensive care in the early
years of a child's life does not mean that the present single
sanctioned form of socialization – marriage and family – is
inevitable. Nor that the mother is the only possible nurse. Far
from it. The fundamental characteristic of the present system
of marriage and family is in our society its *monolithism*; there is

only one institutionalized form of inter-sexual or inter-generational relationship possible. It is that or nothing. This is why it is essentially a denial of life. For all human experience shows that inter-sexual and inter-generational relationships are infinitely various – indeed, much of our creative literature is a celebration of the fact – while the institutionalized expression of them in our capitalist society is utterly simple and rigid. It is the poverty and simplicity of the institutions in this area which are such an oppression. Any society will require some institutionalized and social recognition of personal relationships. But there is absolutely no reason why there should be only one legitimized form – and a multitude of unlegitimized experience. What we should seek for is not the abolition of the family, but the diversification of the socially acknowledged relationships which are today forcibly and rigidly compressed into it. This would mean a plural range of institutions – where the family is only one such institution, and its abolition implies none. Couples – of the same or of different sexes – living together or not living together, long-term unions with or without children, single parents – male or female – bringing up children, children socialized by conventional rather than biological parents, extended kin groups, etc. – all these could be encompassed in a range of institutions which match the free invention and variety of men and women.

This is what we can fight for. Yet today women are confined within the family which is a segmentary, monolithic unit, largely separated off from production and hence from social human activity. The reason why this confinement is made possible is the demand for women to fulfil these three roles: they must provide sexual satisfaction for their partners and give birth to children and rear them. But the family does more than occupy the woman: it produces her. It is in the family that the psychology of men and women is founded. Here is the source of their definition. What is this definition and what is the role of the family in the ideology of it as the basic unit of society today?

Chapter Eight

The Ideology of the Family

The Ideology of the Family

The family as the first form of social organization, has clearly undergone many changes with the advance of the economic methods of production which have always necessitated more and more elaborate social formations to accompany them. In her article 'A Woman's Work is Never Done'[1] Peggy Morton points out that under early capitalism the main economic task of the family was to produce large numbers of children for the new industrial jobs which demanded enormous numbers of workers; but under advanced capitalism, labour-intensive industry gives way to capital-intensive and quality rather than quantity of workers is what is required. The family adapts itself accordingly:

Profits depend more and more on the efficient organization of work and on the 'self-discipline' of the workers rather than simply on speed-ups and other direct forms of increasing the exploitation of the workers. The family is therefore important both to shoulder the burden of the cost of higher education, and to carry out the repressive socialization of children. The family must raise children who have internalized hierarchical social relations, who will discipline themselves and work efficiently without constant supervision.... Women are responsible for implementing most of this socialization.[2]

I agree with Peggy Morton that the way the family is evolving produces an increased number of contradictions for the woman within it. As there is, likewise, a contradiction within the sector of sexuality alone. However, there is also a further

1. Peggy Morton: 'A Woman's Work is Never Done', *Leviathan,* vol. II, no. 1.
2. ibid., p. 34.

crucial contradiction not just within the family, but between it and the social organization that surrounds it. For though the family *has changed* since its first appearance, it *has also remained* – not just an idealist concept but as a crucial ideological and economic unit with a certain rigidity and autonomy despite all its adaptations.

Pre-capitalist society flourishes on individual private property – the peasant has his bit of land, the artisan his tools. Capitalist organization of work deprives the individual of his private property and takes all the separate pieces of private property (land, tools, etc.) pools them, and makes the newly accumulated wealth the private property of a few – the capitalists. The appropriation of individual private property necessitates a form of social organization of the property (men have to get together to work it) which is simultaneously denied: the mass of men get together to work it, but what they produce and how they produce it is taken by the 'few' as their own personal private property. However, individual private property for the mass of the people does continue side by side with this new process – it continues in the family. Engels traced the origin of the oppression of women to the demand for individual private property: women had to be 'owned', faithful to marriage to produce an heir for the inheritance of this individual private property. But perhaps more interesting than the 'origin' of the oppression is its maintenance, as Marx and Engels' analyses of other issues demonstrate. In every revolution (whether from tribalism to feudalism, feudalism to capitalism, capitalism to socialism) the new ruling class, in order to overcome the old ruling class has to *appear* to represent the vast majority of the people in a society (only in the last instance is this *actually* the case): it doesn't, therefore, appear as a particular 'class' but as the whole society:

> For each new class which puts itself in the place of the one ruling before it, is compelled, simply in order to achieve its aims, to represent its interests as the common interest of all the members of society, i.e. employing an ideal formula to give its ideas the form of universality and to represent them as the only rational and

universally valid ones. The class which makes a revolution appears
from the beginning not as a class but as the representative of the
whole of society, simply because it is opposed to a *class*. It appears
as the whole mass of society confronting a single ruling class....
Every new class, therefore, achieves its domination only on a
broader basis than that of the previous ruling class . . .[3]

It is in representing this limited 'class' interest as the
general, universal interest, that 'ideas' play such an important
part. Emergent capitalist society in confronting and overcoming feudal society has to appear to offer what the majority
want – this naturally takes the form of an idealization of what
the previous socio-economic system offered as its basis in,
inevitably, a totally un-ideal manner. The ideas and desires of
all people are conditioned by what they have: they simply want
it bigger and better. To put this concretely – the peasant
masses of feudal society had individual private property; their
ideal was simply more of it. Capitalist society seemed to offer
more because it stressed the *idea* of individual private property
in a new context (or in a context of new ideas). Thus it offered
individualism (an old value) plus the apparently new means for
its greater realization – freedom and equality (values that are
conspicuously absent from feudalism). However, the only
place where this ideal could be given an apparently concrete
base was in the maintenance of an old institution: the family.
Thus the family changed from being the economic basis of
individual private property under feudalism to being the focal
point of the *idea* of individual private property under a system
that banished such an economic form from its central mode of
production – capitalism. In actually owning things, privately
and individually, the bourgeois family gives reality to this
idea. For the rest, it remains an ideal desire – the possible fulfilment of which is an inducement to work in a manner at
logger-heads with it. The working class work socially in
production for the private property of a few capitalists *in the
hope of* individual private property for themselves and their
families.

3. Karl Marx: *The German Ideology,* 1845–6, *Collected Works,* vol. I, iv,
pp. 35–7.

But, of course, the ruling-class interests that pose, in the first place, as universal interests, increasingly decline into 'mere idealizing phrases, conscious illusions and deliberate deceits. ... But the more they are condemned as falsehoods, and the less they satisfy the understanding, the more dogmatically they are asserted and the more deceitful, moralizing and spiritual becomes the language of established society.'[4] Such a state of affairs perfectly describes that of individual private property and its embodiment, the family, towards the end of the nineteenth century in England. During the twentieth century, feudalism having been firmly overcome and capitalism entrenched, the basic ideology remains, but has naturally become more flexible in order to maintain its hold of the reins.

This is not to reiterate the notion that the family had an economic function under feudalism and today under capitalism has only an ideological one. Such a notion misrepresents the specific relationship here between the economic and the ideological and it is further in danger of being interpreted to mean that the family is unnecessary, a part of some con-job. The quotation above which treats ideology from a moral perspective can induce this attitude. There is nothing less 'real' or 'true' or important about the ideological than there is about the economic. Both determine our lives. In any case, the function of the family is not simply one or the other, it is both: it has an economic and ideological role under capitalism. Roughly, the economic role is the provision of a certain type of productive labour-force and of the arena for massive consumption. This is specifically capitalistic. This economic function interacts with the ideology requisite to produce the missing ideals of peasant, feudal society; a place *equally* and *freely* to enjoy individual private property. This ideology which looks backwards for its rationale is, nevertheless, crucial for the present: without it people might hanker back to the past as a 'golden age'; once Utopianism of any sort occurs, after looking backwards, it is liable to look forwards and thus

4. ibid., p. 27. Actually this language remains on the terrain it is attacking – it is ideological language, moral and descriptive rather than analytical. It is, however, elegantly appropriate here.

endanger the status quo. The family, thus, embodies the most conservative concepts available: it rigidifies the past ideals and presents them as the present pleasures. By its very nature, it is there to prevent the future. No wonder revolutionaries come up with the vulgar desperation: abolish the family – it does seem *the* block to advance, *the* means of preserving a backwardness that even capitalism makes feel redundant, though, of course, it is essential to it.

This task of ideology to capture and preserve the ideals that arose from a past reality explains, at least in this context, the degree of separation that exists between the ideological superstructure and the economic base. The ideological construct seems to be less variable, to preserve itself across revolutionary changes in the mode of production. It seems that the values of the present-day family are appropriate to peasant production. But it is the function of the ideology precisely to give this sense of continuity in progress. The dominant ideological formation is not separable from the dominant economic one, but, while linked, it does have a certain degree of autonomy and its own laws. Thus the ideology of the family can remain: individualism, freedom and equality; (at home you're 'yourself'), while the social and economic reality can be very much at odds with such a concept. The contradictions between the ideological intentions of the family and its socio-economic base do not mean that we say the former is false. Quite the contrary, as its meshes draw tighter we protest on behalf of the ideology: 'I can't say a thing without you getting at me.... I'm not free to think my own thoughts.... I've got nothing I can call my own...'

Of course, the ideological concept of the family embodies a paradox which reflects the contradiction between it and the dominant, capitalist method of organizing production. As I have already mentioned, this method of organizing involves social production (a mass or 'team' of workers), and the family provides the relief from the confiscation of this social production by apparently offering individual private property. Now the same contradiction is today contained within the family itself. The family is the most fundamental (the earliest and most primitive) form of social organization. When, under capitalism, it was made to embody as an ideal, what had been its economic function under feudalism, a chronic contradiction took place. What had hitherto been a *united* unit within the overall diversified social structure became, because of changing social conditions, a *divided* one. The peasant family works together for itself – it *is* one. The family and production are homogeneous. But the members of a working-class family work separately, for different bosses in different places and, though the family interest unites them, the separation of their place and conditions of their work fragments, perforce, that unity. Part of the function of the ideology of the family under capitalism is to preserve this unity in the face of its essential break-up. However, in doing this, it ties itself in knots. The social nature of work under capitalism fragments the unitary family; thereby it enforces the social nature of the family itself.

The peasant family owned its individual private property as the family's; but ideological individualism under capitalism cannot relate to a social group (even one as small as the modern family); it must, because it counterposes this to social work, relate to the individual. It is almost as though the family has got smaller and smaller in order to make itself 'one', in a desperate struggle against the disparity of its members in the outside world. Under capitalism, each member of the family is supposed to be 'an individual', it is not the family unit that is individualized. No wonder there are tensions. Each is supposed to be for the other, but every encounter – school, college, work – makes him for himself alone. It is this contradiction between an ideology of the privacy and individuation of the family and its basic social nature, which capitalism by its social organization of work has brought into play, that underlies the psychic problems documented (in England) in the works of the psychiatrists Laing, Esterson, and Cooper. Each member wants to be an individual – but it is the family itself that is supposed to be 'individual'... 'Mary's not like my other children, she's always been different ... she's got a mind of her own and will go places ... she's so stubborn, that's why things went wrong and I've brought her to you, doctor . . .' The woman's task is to hold on to the unity of the family while its separate atoms explode in different directions.

It seems possible that within this dual contradiction lies the eventual dissolution of the 'family', a future already visible within the conditions of capitalism. The social nature of production restores the family to its social form – a social group of individuals. Restores it, in fact, to something like the days before it was a family in little more than the biological sense. But this is only 'something like'; final forms bear a misleading resemblance to postulated original forms – the difference is the entire intervening social development, and the difference between the social groups prior to the private-interest family, and social groups after it, is the difference between 'golden age' primitive communism and revolutionary communism. It is too late for one and high time for the other. Meanwhile, the self-contradictory ideology of the family, which preserves the individualism of the unit only in the increasingly disruptive individualism of its members, both retards and hastens the day.

Chapter Nine

Psychoanalysis and the Family

The Women's Liberation Movement must have a complex reaction to the nuclear family. It must concentrate on separating out the structures – the woman's roles – which are oppressively fused into it. It must fragment its unity.

To do this, we have to examine the concrete role and nature of today's family from within. We have to see precisely what function it serves at all levels. Yet simultaneously we have to see it as a *relatively* constant unit in relation to the entire course of social history. As such, it has a certain autonomy and inflexibility, whatever the stage of economic development of the society as a whole. This is because, in part, it clearly belongs to the ideological superstructure and always has done – even when this coincided with its economic function, as it did with the peasant family: (At the temple) 'people came to burn incense and offer prayers for good fortune, abundant crops, *and many children*'.[1] (my italics)

And...

[... in pre-revolutionary China] very interesting and significant was the factor of family size. The landlords and rich peasants averaged more than five persons per household, the middle peasants fewer than five, the poor peasants, between three and three and a half, the hired labourers about three.... Those without land or with very small holdings were often unable even to marry. If they did marry they were unable to hold their families together, lost more children to disease and famine, had to sell children, or even sell wives, and thus had households about half the size.

1. William Hinton: op. cit., p. 20.

If the landholdings of the pre-revolutionary period were calculated on the basis of the number of families rather than per
capita, the concentration of wealth in the hands of the landlords and
rich peasants was more marked. On that basis – a very realistic one
for China, where the *traditional emphasis has always been on the family*
rather than on *the individual* – the landlords and rich peasants, with
only 5 per cent of the families, controlled 31 per cent of the land. . .[2]

Today, the ideological function clearly still relates to the
economic function – though both have changed at different
rates and an important dislocation has resulted.

If we undertake only the first analysis, the meaning of the
family, or of women's roles, we get sociology – the type of
research that has littered the academic bookshelves of the
anglo-saxon world (significantly) in the last decade. If we
study only the place of the family within capitalist society, we
get mere idealism for we fall into the trap of seeing it as an
abstract concept:

> The family, which is at first the only social relationship, becomes
> later, when increased needs create new social relations and the
> increased population new needs, a subordinate one ... and must
> then be treated and analysed according to the existing empirical
> data, not according to the 'concept of the family'.[3]

Yes and no. A political study of the family, crucial to the
development of the Women's Liberation Movement, involves the double approach: both the empirical data and the
structure and importance of the ideological concept: the
family itself in its 'conceptual' unitary form.

The Family 'makes' the Woman

We are concerned primarily with the implications of the
capitalist family for the woman enmeshed within it. On one
level, women in today's family, are the main repositories for
what are coming to seem the screaming illusions of our

2. ibid., p. 28. This makes two of my points at once – the coincidence of
economic need and ideological attitude and the feudal stress on the
individual family – rather than the capitalist stress on the individual person.
3. *The German Ideology*: op. cit., pp. 18–19.

society: freedom, equality, individuality. 'My wife and I are equals' is the correlate of 'the two sides of industry'. 'Equality' and 'sides' suggest a faint line drawn down the *middle*. In both cases there is a topside and a bottom side, an unequal division of labour and an unequal division of profits – to put it mildly.

The family is a stronghold of what capitalism needs to preserve but actually destroys: private property and individualism. The housewife-mother is the guardian and representative of these. She is a backward, conservative force – and this is what her oppression means. She is forced to be the stone in the stream. Her work is private and *because it is private*, and for no other reason, it is unsupervised. This is the source of that complacent 'Your time's your own, you are your own boss' mystifying build-up that housewives are given. For every process of production that involves combined social forces and cooperation (enforced or voluntary) also requires superintendence or direction; it is only *isolated* labour that is free from this need. The 'freedom' of the housewife is her isolation.

The Effects of Oppression

Working alone, grappling with the vestiges of individual property, women in the family are used to deflect the tide and implications of social labour. Out of the increasingly numerous contradictions of their position, a sense of their oppression is growing ever stronger. From this can come the revolutionary impulse to overthrow it. But we must not neglect the marks that oppression has left us with.

Just as, on the one hand, it is crucial that we are never guilty of underestimating the potential of women, so we must never neglect to be aware of the difficulties of our position. In a different context (that of military struggle) Mao called going it alone and underestimating the difficulties 'Left Sectarianism' and underestimating one's potential and fearing to struggle 'Right Opportunism'. On the one hand, we have to dare to struggle, dare to win: on the other, we have to treat the struggle seriously. In the Women's Liberation Movement we have (at least in the United States), made the initial move possible, but if we don't correctly estimate the difficulties we will be guilty of 'Left Sectarianism' – a voluntarism that will be at least a temporary death knell.

The difficulties that confront us are not just the opposition of the system we are confronting, but also its influence. It is this latter difficulty that I think we are in danger of ignoring. The conditions of our oppression *do* condition us. And we have to assess the weakness of women as a political force in order *not* to succumb to it. The Women's Liberation Movement is directed at all women – we have to know what we are asking.

What does our oppression within the family *do* to us women? It produces a tendency to small-mindedness, petty jealousy, irrational emotionality and random violence, dependency, competitive selfishness and possessiveness, passivity, a lack of vision and conservatism. These qualities are *not* the simple produce of male chauvinism, nor are they falsely ascribed to women by a sexist society that uses 'old woman' as a dirty term. *They are the result of the woman's objective conditions within the family* – itself embedded in a sexist society. You cannot inhabit a small and backward world without it doing something to you. Peasants, as a potential revolutionary force, present comparable problems. Their whole life having been based on personal struggles for a little land and beating each other's prices in the market-place, makes revolutionary solidarity hard for them and the tendency to divisive and selfish seizure of individual gain, a difficult one to combat. Women, likewise, have always competed for the best men, the nicest home, the most successful kids; it is hard for them to come together as a socialized political force when the conditions of their lives are set to exclude this possibility. The working class is the revolutionary class under capitalism, because it engages in *socially* organized work, in this society in an antagonistic form which in turn makes clear to it that it must overthrow this form to release its social potential – socialism. This does not mean that oppressed peoples have no revolutionary potential – their oppression guarantees that. But the nature of the oppression does determine some of the difficulties of their struggle.

Though 'women are wonderful' and 'Black is beautiful' are crucial elements in the 'dare to struggle, dare to win' stage, they must go hand in hand with a knowledge of what our oppression has done to retard us. It is in understanding this latter aspect that radical feminism seems to me to fall down. If men are the oppressors rather than, say, men in particular roles, such as father and husband, acting as agents of the objective oppression, then all we have to do is to overturn these oppressed characteristics and we will be liberated. The struggle would be much easier – because it is impossible. To say that women have none (or need have none) of the above-listed negative feminine characteristics is moralism not politics. And it is engaging battle on the terrain of moralism: 'There have never been any great women artists. . . . Yes, there have, you just didn't notice them or you never let us be. . . . I dedicate this book to my wife without whose stoical patience and endless assistance . . . shut up.' Well, that's alright as rhetoric, and rhetoric and anger have their place – but that place is *within* political strategy, not in place of strife.

Psychology, Psychoanalysis and Empiricism

It is, then, the effects of the family on women that have to be studied. One of the most crucial of these effects is on the psychology of its members. Radical feminism postulates a primary psychological demand for power by men as the original source of the oppression of women. In doing this, it confirms what is, to me, a serious error in our movement – it simplifies psychology and is content with a rejection of psychoanalysis for its dislikeable ideology. The American Movement's rejection of Freud, in particular, is a further manifestation of the moral response to the negative feminine attributes I have detailed.[4]

4. This is unfair to Shulamith Firestone's very interesting account of Freud's importance in *The Dialectics of Sex:* op. cit. It is particularly unfair

The mistake largely originates from the post-Freudian analysts themselves, and from a confusion between psychoanalysis and psychology and psychiatry. All three have reduced Freud's discovery of a science to vulgar empiricism. It is mostly in these terms that the women's liberationists have naturally responded.

There is no doubt that the ideology that Freud's followers picked up from Freud, and made into their 'theory' is pernicious to women and should be forcefully combated. It is also pernicious to psychoanalysis. A paradigmatic case of this is the contribution of the Princess Marie Bonaparte in her work *Female Sexuality*:

> On the other hand, it would generally appear that, if the girl is to become a true woman, her phallic masturbation, normal up to the castration complex, *must* succumb even more to the biological castration complex than to educative prohibitions, and that the female vagina, erotized at puberty, must then be passively content to *await* the male penis that will awaken it. For the role of everything female, from the ovum to the beloved is a waiting one. The vagina must await the advent of the penis in the same passive, latent and dormant manner that the ovum awaits the spermatozoon. Indeed the eternally feminine myth of *The Sleeping Beauty* is the retelling of that first biological relation.[5]

Each page of the book is more monstrous than the last – it becomes quite fun to read it, until she describes an operation she practised to displace the clitoris of frigid women. Amazingly, it didn't work. Imagine engrafting a penis on the middle of an impotent man's belly. But if Bonaparte and her ilk have landed us in the mire of empiricism, it is pointless to engage in

in the light of the fact that she was one of the originators of radical feminism. Perhaps I can amend this, without altering the point I am making, by saying that radical feminists, by reducing the oppression of women to psychological warfare *do* reduce both oppression and psychology, but they also take both seriously. I should also point out that although both Firestone and myself evaluate Freud highly, we do so from opposite positions. For me the value of psychoanalysis is as a science; for Firestone it is '. . . poetic rather than scientific; (Freud's) ideas are more valuable as metaphors than as literal truths'. (p. 52).

5. Marie Bonaparte: *Female Sexuality*, Evergreen, 1965, p. 57.

combat *on the same terms*. If the post-Freudians conned us into thinking we are having vaginal orgasms – it's very useful that Masters and Johnson have put us right. But its usefulness is as far as it goes. After all one can have an orgasm just by thinking about it. For every piece of research offered by experimental psychology you could spend centuries confirming or counteracting it. As far as experiments with attitudes to women are concerned, this has a certain rallying value as counterideology – but no more than this. Thus Naomi Weisstein's article 'Psychology Constructs the Female'[6] describes how attitudes of researchers condition the response of the 'researched upon' (even when they are rats) and thus investigations into women's behaviour discover 'womanly' behaviour. But we should use this, not to feel outraged at the stupidity of the experiments (though they certainly are that), but to see the importance and pervasiveness of ideology. Again, it's fun to know that if people are told a piece of writing is by a man they think it is excellent, and if they are told it is by a woman, it is 'poor to indifferent'. But don't we know it already? Aren't such attitudes essential to our oppression. If we believe we are oppressed, do we need such details, except to convince those who don't believe we are. . . . They are the illustrations of our theory, not its substance.

Naomi Weisstein makes a plea for understanding the individual personality in the context of his or her social environment. This is clearly important.[7] Relevantly, from our point of view, this is the aim of the analyses of the family, pursued by the psychotherapists Laing, Cooper and Esterson. In studying inter-personal relationships they have given psychological documentation and insight into the generation-gap. In doing this, they have been both a symptom of, and ideologues for, the Youth Movements. The Women's Liberation

6. Dr Naomi Weisstein: '"Kinde, Küche, Kirche" as Scientific Law: Psychology constructs the Female', reprinted in *Sisterhood is Powerful*, ed. Robin Morgan, Random House, 1970. (A most useful anthology.)

7. One could point out that Freud's case studies are models of analysis of the patient's environment. See, for instance, 'Dora: A Fragment of an Analysis of a Case Study of Hysteria', 1905, *Collected Works*, vol. VII, for an early example and a case history of a woman patient.

Movement has naturally inherited this analysis along with its attendant values and, in doing so, has possibly missed out on the fact that, rich as it is in understanding inter-generational conflict, so is it poor in even noticing inter-sexual tensions.

So far neither the psychiatrists of the family, nor those of the sexual revolution (Reich), nor post-Freudian Anglo-Saxon analysts, have offered much of interest about women. This is not true of Freud's own work, nor is it true of the possibilities of the science he originated.

Freud and Psychoanalysis

First of all, it is important for us to understand the implications of psychoanalysis as a science. Naomi Weisstein comments:

> In *The Sexual Enlightenment of Children*, the classic document which is supposed to demonstrate empirically the existence of a castration complex and its connection to a phobia, Freud based his analysis on the reports of the father of the little boy, himself in therapy, and a devotee of Freudian theory. I really don't have to comment further on the contamination in this kind of evidence. . . . Years of intensive clinical experience is not the same thing as empirical evidence.[8]

It is not, and it was never meant to be. This argument supposes that all sciences are tested in the same way – the way of the natural sciences. But on the contrary, a new science explores a new terrain and has new, appropriate methods of proof. As Freud put it:

> What characterizes psycho-analysis as a science is not the material which it handles but the technique with which it works . . . what it aims at and achieves is nothing other than the uncovering of what is unconscious in mental life.[9]

The same tendency towards empirical validation that marks Naomi Weisstein's contention is present in the post-Freudian

8. Weisstein: op. cit., pp. 209–10.
9. Sigmund Freud: Introductory Lectures, XXIV, 'The Common Neurotic State', 1916–17, *Collected Works*, vol. XVI, p. 389.

interpretation of 'the cure'. The last thing Freud meant this to be was the adaptive process prevalent today.[10] He saw psychoanalysis as revolutionary, shocking, subversive – a plague that would disrupt society. In this conviction (a conviction inherent in the development of a new science) he equalled that other great scientific discovery of the nineteenth century – Marxist political economy – dialectical and historical materialism.

Psychoanalysis, exploring the unconscious and the constructs of mental life, works on the terrain of which the dominant pehomenal form is the family. In studying women we cannot neglect the methods of a science of the mind, a theory that attempts to explain how women become women and men, men. The borderline between the biological and the social which finds expression in the family is the land that psychoanalysis sets out to chart, it is the land where sexual distinction originates. That Freud, personally, had a reactionary ideological attitude to women in no way affects his science – it wouldn't be a science if it did. That he partook of the social mores and ideology of his time whilst he developed a science that could overthrow them is neither a contradiction nor a limitation of his work. As he, himself, said: 'My life is of no interest except in its relation to psychoanalysis . . .'[11]

It is post-Freudian empiricism that has trapped most of Freud's tentative analyses of sexual differences into a crude and offensive rigidity. Notorious concepts such as 'penis envy' have come to suggest to most people a wish to seize the object itself. But what underlies this concept is, in fact, Freud's much more complex notion of the power of the image of the phallus within human society. It is its social, ideological and psychic power, embodied in the thing itself. It is this basic distinction and relationship between the idea and its object (not in the Platonic sense) that is crucial to psychoanalytic theory and that, missed, leads to all the absurdities of empirical refutation.

10. See, what is to me faraway the best brief presentation of Freud available in English that I know of, Octave Mannoni: *Freud,* Pantheon Books, 1970.

11. Sigmund Freud. Quoted by Mannoni: op. cit., p. 8.

Thus, for example, Freud traced the omnipresent sense of guilt to the image of the father in a person's (and a society's) life; a manifestation of this was the prohibition on childhood masturbation – the fact that 'progressively' brought up children are today allowed to masturbate, in no way invalidates this, in no way mitigates the overall sense of guilt, and in no way detracts from masturbation's *symbolic* meaning. That infants now usually see their mother naked, doesn't prevent their theories that she once had a penis and is now castrated – what counts is the significance (determined by, *not* the limited social context, but by the context that all human beings form societies) that all babies and, for that matter, all people, give to *absence*, as such.

The empiricist's adaptations and refutations have been disastrous for the initial, and partial moves Freud made into an understanding of sexual differences. It is not just that they have taken his postulates as solutions, but that also they have demanded of his science something that it is not within its nature to give. It's like asking Newton what the air pressure did to the apple as it fell. What Newton was scientifically investigating was gravity not the decomposition of fruit. If the former enables us to find out about the latter – well and good, but it is not its task.

Freud wrote:

.... in conformity with its peculiar nature, psychoanalysis does not try to describe what a woman is – that would be a task it could scarcely perform – but sets about enquiring how she comes into being, how a woman develops out of a child with a bisexual disposition.[12]

If we don't want to know how a woman 'comes into being' let's leave Freud's science alone – but, at least, don't let's use it and abuse it to tell us 'what a woman is', when its own territory, its own method, and its own originator, expressly prohibit our doing so.

However, to ignore Freud is like ignoring Marx – it reveals

12. Sigmund Freud: New Introductory Lectures, XXXIII, 'Femininity', 1933, *Collected Works*, vol. XXII, p. 116.

a preference for pre-scientific ideology over scientific discovery. Ptolemy still has poetic truth on his side – the sun
rising in the east *seems* to move across our sky. The Women's
Liberation Movement cannot afford to indulge the bad poetry
about women, when we have a science we can use, explore,
criticize, amend. For psychoanalysis, like all sciences, is open
not closed. Freud was dying of cancer when he offered his
most familiar analyses of the formation of a woman, these are
all we have that is specific – but the whole field of the science
is ours to develop.

Freud discovered the crucial importance of the social construction of the human animal; that this bio-sexual interpretation of the anatomical-biological made the person a person,
constructed the mind, the conscious and unconscious. This
social interpretation occurs both individually and, con-
comitantly, generically; the human animal does not become a
human being just at the moment of his birth – he became so
hundreds of thousands of years ago. The personal life history,
the entire human cultural heritage (general and specific) and
the biological destiny of anatomy interact. The arena for their
interaction is the pattern of primary relationships which,
usually but not necessarily, are secondarily expressed in the
family. This pattern of relationships and its implications in
human culture, as we have so far known it, he called the
Oedipal situation. This comprises two parents of the opposite
sex and their relationship to each other and their offspring, and
its to them. Again, for the sake of the empiricists, it doesn't
matter if the child is adopted at birth: this pattern is as inherent in our culture as it is in our biology. Freud analysed the
implications of this pattern. That he worked in a patriarchal
culture, of course, determined his findings, but then to date
most human beings have been formed in patriarchal cultures.
It is us, not just Freud, who are thus determined. The presence
of matrilineal or matrifocal societies does not really contradict
this: they are marginal, undocumented psychoanalytically, and
we don't really know the meaning given to the presence of the
father. For whatever the legal – or customary – situation, the
'idea' of the father could still be very dominant, and we must

remember there always *is* a father and it is the *idea* of him that Freud was commenting on.

In the classic Oedipal situation, the boy loves and stifles his love for his mother, hates his father as rival for his mother, and buries his hatred by identifying with the object of it. One day he too will be a father and have his own woman (mother-wife). The girl loves her father and hates her mother as rival, but she does not have to suppress this as forcefully as the boy does. She can imitate her mother (as the boy can his father) and continue to flirt with her father (as the boy *can't* with his mother). The boy can't continue to desire his mother because he realizes his penis can't compete with that of his father. He fears castration. But the girl discovers that she can't be castrated as she hasn't a penis to offer, but then neither has her mother – there's not much to choose between them. The girl will thus grow up *like* her mother but the boy will grow up to be *another* father. The girl has little need to leave the Oedipal scene. Now this presupposes two things (both of which concerned Freud): (1) a fundamental heterosexual urge that makes one sex want the other sex, (2) that the idea of the phallus is the most powerful of all in the formation of society. But, in any case, it is in the Oedipal situation that the anatomical female is set on the path of her social destiny of womanhood, and the male of manhood. And it is the different ways (and degrees) in which the boy and the girl move out of it that determines so many of their characteristics. Relevantly here, in the case of women, these link up with their negative oppressed behavioural qualities described earlier.

Late in his life, Freud decided that the Oedipal moment didn't happen at a specific time (say, two years old) but extended backwards and forwards to the entry (or rather, numerous entries) of any foetus or infant into human society. It is this area of transition (and mingling) from the biological given to the social interpretation that is the subject of psychoanalysis; it is this area where the infant with specific male or female sex organs, yet retaining a bisexual disposition (could develop, that is, with the social-sexual characteristics of either sex), nevertheless becomes socialized (or humanized) according to one possibility, the one that it is felt corresponds with its anatomy.

It is this area that any analysis of the position and meaning of women has to explore. Reactionary ideology always returns us to our biological fate (smaller equals weaker, child-bearing equals animal, etc.). We cannot simply say: 'But it's the meaning society gives to this that matters – it is this that we will challenge and change.' For this meaning is given with our very entry into society; it is, indeed, coincident with society.

Psychoanalysis explores the primary interrelationships between individual animals that make them human beings. By its very definition it is an analysis of the most basic social formation – that which finds its expression in the various forms of family:

> It follows from the nature of the facts which form the material of psycho-analysis that we are obliged to pay as much attention in our case histories to the purely human and social circumstances of our patients as to the somatic data and the symptoms of the disorder. Above all, our interest will be directed towards their family circumstances – and not only, as will be seen later, for the purpose of enquiring into their heredity.[13]

Conclusions and Comments on Chapters Six, Eight and Nine

Our analysis of the family has to proceed on three fronts. The germ of the family is the source of the psychic creation of individuals; this 'germ' has certain universal characteristics – heterosexual parents and offspring (see Chapter 9). The dominant ideology of the family gives its very various forms and functions an atemporality and a permanence (the ideology creates a continuity by its backward-lookingness whereby the present family encapsulates values that were the ideals of previous systems). (See Chapter 8.) The economic function of the family gives it its specific highly temporal form: that this function is ensured success by the role played by ideology

13. Sigmund Freud: 'Dora', op. cit., p. 18.

within the family – the inculcated obedience of children, sub-servience of the wife, etc. – should not be confused with the ideological concept of the family as such, the dominant ideology just mentioned (see Chapter 6). The bio-social universal, the ideological atemporal, the economic specificity all interlock in a complex manner; the interrelationship of these elements demand that we understand each of them. Psychoanalysis, the scientific method for investigating the first, can be neglected no more than scientific socialism for understanding the last, the economic, and both are needed for developing a comprehension of the ideological.

Chapter Ten

Out From Under . . .

Comments and Conclusions

The Women's Liberation Movement arose in the second half of the sixties through the combined impact of two different forces. The first force is the contradictions that came to the surface within the position of women in advanced capitalist society.

Women's position in society is in the home – and outside it, in production. Their place in production alone is replete with contradictions. They are in the most advanced and the most backward economic sectors. Men are in *all* sectors, according to class. Women are crucial for the expansion of consumer-consciousness (e.g. their use as 'sexual objects' by the advertising industry), yet they are also a permanent source of the *cheapest* labour for use in the conventional early capitalist industries, (see, for instance, conditions in English wool mills). There is a contradiction between their position in production and an ideology that virtually excludes them from it, (most people don't realize how many women are out at work). This is the contradiction between their role in the family and their role in the labour-force: the one denies the other. Then the family itself contains the contradictions of its ideology (which stabilizes it) and of its economic function (which changes it). Within the family, the reproduction and the socialization of children are made to balance each other, yet ever more precariously: contraception and the population explosion indicate the possibility, and need, for fewer births; psychology makes the period of early infancy crucial; the woman must spend the energy freed from child-birth in child-rearing. Yet with compulsory schooling, early maturing, for how long is a full-time mother really required? Probably just so long as she is denied the social possibilities (day-care, economic independence, etc.) that would give her the option. In sexuality itself there is a contradiction: women are enjoying a new sexual freedom (changing moral attitudes and availability of reliable contraception) but this is often only for their greater exploitation as 'sexual objects' within it. The explosive possibilities of sexual freedom and the more lax attitudes to marriage which *could* undermine the family are made never to do so – at least for the woman, who is nearly always left holding the baby. As there is always a contradiction between the manner in which women are maintained (even in the lowest income groups) and their personal poverty, the new notional liberation of sexuality and laxity of marriage most often frees women only into insecurity – economic as much as emotional. It cannot be overstressed how the lack of potential economic independence even of working women preserves the family against all odds. Marriage is a 'life-long union'. But until this century, with later marriages and earlier deaths, this could mean no more than twenty years – of which fifteen were spent producing and rearing children. Today the children have usually left home before the marriage is even half way through. The man must go on earning hard to 'support' his wife in the absence of his once dependent children. The sexual tensions of the predicament are often more visible than the economic absurdities: in the Victorian couple, the wife did not expect satisfaction, she was usually pregnant, and sexual prowess was allowed to decline steeply with age. Today, diet and psychology enable sexual potency and desire in both man and woman till death do us part. The rising divorce rate may be less due to the decrease in the stability of marriage than to the increase in life-expectancy.

These then, are some of the contradictions in the position of women within their world – the family; and within – 'it's a man's world; – the economy. These factors doubtless caused the resurgence of feminism. But its specific timing and particular characteristics (its revolutionary potential) are also the result of a second force: the preceding and concurrent political movements of the sixties.

Black Power, Student, Youth and Peace Movements all embodied values that, in one way or another, easily found expression in Women's Liberation. In the United States, black women found themselves the most oppressed within and without their race: their political movement would only recognize their position if *they* did. But of greatest importance to Women's Liberation, Black Power focussed on general oppression rather than on economic exploitation alone, and it validated separatist politics. The new politics of all the youth movements extolled and rediscovered subjectivity, the relevance of emotionality and the need for personal freedom and respect for that of others. Subjectivity, emotionality, a 'caring' for others had previously tended to be designated 'feminine' qualities. Ironically the counter-culture expressed itself by giving prominence to values hitherto downgraded – 'womanly' ones, 'Make love not war' – the personal takes precedence – as it has always had to do for women. 'Togetherness' and 'do your own thing' – fates to which women had long been condemned in the suffocation of the family and the isolation of the home – were now given a different meaning. That these female values were appropriated by male radicals initially gave women hope within these movements. But when they found even here, where their oppressed characteristics seemed to be the order of the day, they played a secondary (to be generous) role, righteous resentment was rampant.

The situation that produced the so-called generation gap in the early sixties, and the subsequent youth movements, shares some of the same contradictions that produced the Women's Liberation Movement. The cult of youth and a reverence for its joys is to be matched with a scene of real economic deprivation. For young people who leave school at fifteen there is serious unemployment (in Britain and the North American continent) and wages are extremely low. We honour the early physical maturing by dropping the legal age of maturation from twenty-one to eighteen years old and, at the same time, both from pressures of the economic situation and from those of ideological attitudes, we force these 'mature' people to remain in highly 'immature' institutions for as long as possible – in schools or colleges. If they refuse, we do not pay them a living wage so they are forced to continue to live in their parent's home long after their emotional and sexual experience has leapt the bounds of the normal family repressions. Kept in the institutions of childhood – the family and/or the school – long after maturity, told that youth is freedom and power, and yet unable to find even the basic means for realizing these – an adequately paid job – young people in the seventies find themselves trapped in the dilemma that likewise embraces women: the contradiction between the ideology of their freedom and a real economic deprivation that makes the ideology a farce. It is not, then, that students are the 'new poor', nor indeed that youth in general are poor that is relevant: it is the contradiction between the assumptions in which they are embedded and the economic conditions which mock them, that has produced much of their radical awareness.

A great deal of the radical protest has taken the form of a demand for the realization of the gifts we are supposed to be enjoying anyway. The demand for personal freedom finds expression in the drug-culture, the drop-out syndrome, the new forms of living-style, etc. The demand to enjoy the rights, the privileges and the maturity which the ideology appears already to accord them underlies the students' wish for participation in the running of the university. If the society says we are so lucky, so mature, etc., let's see it – let's try to get the things it says we've already got. In the event, taking what we are supposed to have, proves a pretty radical activity. The policeman steps in to tell us, we are, after all, supposed to live by faith alone.

Women's Liberation is no exception to this general pattern. In our society women are supposed to be equal. O.K., so let's see it. And they find – like the adolescents with their vaunted 'freedom' – that the more equal they are supposed to be, the more actual is their inequality.

Of course, freedom, equality and the rights of the individual are the fundamental ideologies of a 'free enterprise' economy. In a system which in fact allows none, all are synonymous. It is interesting, too, that all are the obverse of what does, and must prevail. The three qualities in which we 'believe' most are the three qualities most determinedly banished from capitalist society, whose economy is predicated on the *unequal* distribution of wealth and ownership and from which all lack of freedom and of possibility for the realization of individuality follows as night the day.

The 'new politics' of the late sixties and seventies start by engaging at this ideological level. They ask for a realization of the myths that society offers. Too often they have got stuck in the absurdity they are challenging; too often have they pretended to find these values. This is the danger of ideological warfare, divorced from the economic reality that it is there to mask. In a hippy commune you can think you've found freedom, equality and individualism – it is this the communes have died from, not drugs and violence. They were condemned to death the moment they believed in what they were doing; the drug they swallowed was to trust that the ideological promises of capitalist society would be valid if only they could be realized. They forgot that the struggle for these values meant a struggle against a system that prevented, by its definition, their realization.

Women are at the centre of this ideological contradiction. The Women's Liberation Movement has demanded, alongside the youth movement, the validation of certain qualities and, at the same time, because these qualities have been oppressed in their previous forms, they have been counteracted. Thus, on the one hand, we build up feminine virtues to have a status in a male supremacist world – we are kindly, soft-spoken, inward looking – believing these to be women's contributions to 'human nature' – but where these same values have been abused we will overcome them, so we will learn self-defence and aggression. There is nothing wrong with this instinct – except that that is all it is. Similarly in trying to organize around our own values, we try not to imitate the style and structure of male-dominated radical groups. The refusal to allow leaders to arise is the most obvious aspect of this. A good instinct this – nevertheless it presents problems. It is a moral rather than a political decision and has developed out of a desire to preserve moral values rather than to establish a revolutionary organization. This is dangerous because, not yet having any theoretical scientific base from which to understand the oppression of women, it leaves us vulnerable to the return of our own repressed, oppressed characteristics. Already in America many of the liberationists and feminists who were active and dominant last year are invisible this – the fear of leadership accusations makes many people retreat from their own potential. What often is operating is not the politics of democracy but the psychology of envy. People who want to be where others are, make certain the place is kept empty. 'Leaders' are rarely ousted by anyone other than would-be leaders. In not wishing to act like 'men', there is no need for us to act like 'women'. The rise of the oppressed should not be a glorification of oppressed characteristics – such a process would be jumping onto the roundabout of a vicious circle.

This is, I believe the danger the movement faces at the moment. The danger of moral and not political advances confronts us from all directions. 'Consciousness-raising' within the small group *can* turn round on itself and become a self-repeating, incestuous personal-problem session: 'male chauvinism' as a concept can simply be used to evade the relationship of men and women within our society and as part of a 'more-oppressed-than-thou' campaign.[1] Feminism, which postulates the primacy of sexual oppression over all other

1. The same moral competitiveness is often to be found in the arguments of left-wing opponents of Women's Liberation: working-class men are having a far tougher time than middle-class women. I asked a friend, mother of six children, with a family income of £18 per week whether she thought financial or sexual inequalities were the greatest. After some thought, she said that being a woman was the most unequal thing. It's a hard question to answer. *And it doesn't really matter.* Exploitation need not vie with oppression; revolutionary potential does not crudely follow the graph of deprivation.

forms, has no scientific theory for this assumption: nothing really explains why it arose, why and how it continued and, hence nothing comes to mind as to how it is to be overcome. If the psychological power compulsion of men originated it, what originated that – and what can supersede it, other than the psychological power-compulsion of women? A tit-for-tat psycho-moral solution.

Profound contradictions in the position of women caused the rise of the movement; it is these that have to be studied if a political strategy is to be evolved. Engels thought that the precondition for the liberation of women was their introduction into the industrial economy – the paid, labour force. With women as 42 per cent of the United States labour force, the 'precondition' has all but been achieved; but at a moment when the composition of the labour force and the demands of capitalist industry are somewhat different from those found in the mid-nineteenth century. Imperialism has enabled the transformation of the most profitable industries in the home-country from labour-intensive industries to capital-intensive-ones. But women, like workers in the Third World colonies (or ex-colonies) and like workers in the early capitalist societies, are in the labour-intensive areas. Wages are bound to be kept low, because they are a heavy item in the overall expenditure. Women are, then, probably the most exploited sector of the work-force. But this exploitation as part of the working class is made invisible by their identification with the other aspect of their condition – their oppression as wives within the family. Here they join all classes of women to work – from an economic point of view – in a pre-capitalist mode of production. Here they are more analogous to peasants under feudalism. As, for instance, in pre-revolutionary China there were 'rich', 'middle' and 'poor' peasants, so there are 'rich', 'middle' and 'poor' housewives. These categories constitute different economic and social status within the group (women or peasants). Because that group's relationship within the overall system is an oppressed one, the group as a whole (whatever the sub-group) is potentially revolutionary – though the 'rich' are unlikely to identify with the group, and though the 'middle' have far less to gain than the 'poor', they do have something – the overthrow of the oppressed status.[2]

The analogy is by no means perfect.[3] If any analogy could be, there would be no need for us to work on understanding the position of women. I have used it, however, because I think it leads us to the complexity at the heart of the class position of women. In employment, women are of a class – mostly the working class. But this can rarely lead to class-consciousness for two basic reasons: (1) This does not involve economic independence, (2) Their primary identification is as *maintained* persons within the family. Without the belief that they should earn an independent living wage, women find it hard even to develop trade-union consciousness and a sense of the right to fight for one. Everything beyond this is clearly impossible: women, in these economic conditions (and all the ideological mystifications that go with them) can only move to a class-conscious position behind their men. *And that is not a class-conscious position.* Clearly, then, their entry into the work-force is not enough: *they must enter in their own right and with their own independent economic interest.*

This is not possible, because on the one hand, the economy uses them as cheap labour and, on the other, they have a social, economic and ideological role to play in the family. Though women in advanced capitalist countries form a high percentage of the work-force, they are not *half* this force. When we think which are the women that are *excluded* from the work-force, the problem presents itself in a new light. It is, on the one hand, prosperous middle-class women and, on the other, women of all classes with young children; these latter women are largely in their early twenties. The first category are women in the dominant, hegemonic class in capitalist society, their absence from the labour-force is crucial for the

2. The 'rich' women or peasants are unlikely to feel any identification with their generic category. They are much more likely to identify with the dominant class – landlords or upper class and hence to resist any revolutionary possibilities evoked from the group below them.

3. For a different analogy between women and peasants see Margaret Benston: 'The Political Economy of Women's Liberation', *Monthly Review*, vol. XXI, 4 September 1969, pp. 13–28.

position of women; they and their class are the most prominent producers of the social ideologies that enmesh all women. The other category is no less crucial, though very different. These women – the vast majority – are excluded from the work-force at the most formative period of their lives from the point of view of the development of class-consciousness. It has always been pointed out by professional women that their absence from work at this juncture has blighted their careers (they get out of touch, particularly in the sciences; they miss the years of promotion, etc.) but the significance of working-class women's absence from work in their twenties is not seen as important: they are lucky to be out of it. In fact, it is critical: being in unskilled jobs, it is not that they miss increments, the development of skills, etc. but that it is in this age group that commitment to union militancy evolves. This period is the period of adult psychic and political formation. For the working-class woman despite her past and future, this moment is determined *outside the labour force; outside a situation of potential class-consciousness* – it is determined in the home. The situation of women is, in this respect, unique. In no other class, race, immigrant group, oppressed or otherwise, are both the people from the dominant sector (the bourgeoisie under capitalism) permanently outside the social work-force, *and* the people from the largest and the revolutionary class excluded from the labour-force (the condition that makes them the revolutionary class) in the crucial years. The simple entry of women into the labour force in massive numbers, whether under socialism or capitalism, cannot substantially alter the position. Denied the possibility of economic independence, excluded from the pos-sibility of autonomous development of class-consciousness by this and by the absence from work in the formative years, women's participation as a huge sector of the working-class work force remains merely a painful and arduous formality. The absence of the dominant class, bourgeois women, com-pounds the socio-economic implications of this by adding to them an ideology that confirms them. At a time when for social reasons (lack of alternative provisions for children) virtually all women *have* to be at home, the ideology of the leisured classes tells them that that is where they should be anyway. The spider's web is dense as well as intricate ... come into my parlour and be a true woman.

In the home the social function and the psychic identity of women as a group is found. Class differences at work (which anyway never produce class-consciousness) are here obliterated for status differences: 'wealthy', 'middling', 'poor'. This is not to underestimate these. But the position of women as women takes precedence: oppressed whatever their particular circumstances. Hence the importance of feminist consciousness in any revolution .... Hence Woman's Liberation.

JULIET MITCHELL was born in New Zealand in 1940. She came to England in 1944 and was educated at King Alfred School, London. She read English as an exhibitioner at St. Anne's College, Oxford, where she was a postgraduate student. From 1962 until 1970 she lectured in English literature, first at Leeds and then at Reading University.

She is one of the editors of the *New Left Review* and a member of the London Women's Liberation Workshop. In addition to literary articles, she has also written and lectured extensively in England, Scandinavia, Canada, and the United States, on women and women's liberation. She is at present working full-time on a book on women and the family.

VINTAGE WORKS OF SCIENCE
AND PSYCHOLOGY